A DEADLY DAY IN THE LIFE OF AN AMERICAN AGENT IN MEXICO

ELIAS CAMACHO

This book is dedicated to all those law enforcement officers who have given the ultimate in service to their communities, for their strong dedication and belief in what they were doing. And to all of those who have served and those who are still serving with great dedication to the preservation and safety of their country and its citizens. To all of those who have proudly worn the many different uniforms of peace keepers and who remained faithful to the principals, dedication, honor, and discipline of law enforcement, no matter in what country they served.

I also dedicate this book to a very dear friend who has been with me throughout and who encouraged me to write this book. Al without your help this book would have never been possible. Thank you Doctor Al Marcelo for your encouragement, suggestions and patience.

A special thanks to my Son, Marco A. Camacho for creating the cover.

Table of Contents

Foreword

102, 696 Homicides. 45,000 troops. 2% convictions. Those were the number of people who were killed in Mexico from 2006-2012; As well as the number of soldiers that patrol the streets of the country daily; Followed by the percentage of successful homicide investigations that lead to convictions. Just south of the border lies a country that has become so dangerous, that the most high profile criminals operate with impunity and are allowed to go free, in what are called prison "escapes."

Can you imagine 45,000 American soldiers patrolling the streets of the United States?

Can you imagine 102, 696 Americans killed from homicide in a 6 year period?

Yet still, that is the reality of our nearest southern neighbor. These are the circumstances that Detective Eli Camacho operated in during his duty as an American Agent operating in Mexico. This American Hero who served his country in the US Navy aboard the USS Constellation during the Viet Nam war, and later as a Police Detective, took on the tall order of working the Mexican side of the border, in the Car Theft Division.

Some of his experiences are included in this book, and they will fascinate you. And spark a jolt of adrenaline right through your system.

When Detective Camacho started to share some of these

experiences with me, I knew that he had to share this with the world. To remind the world what a complicated, corrupt, and crime ridden Country Mexico had become.

The closest I could force myself to compare some of the drama unfolding on the Mexican landscape, were the days of the Wild West, when bandits like Billy the Kid ran free. But even Billy was eventually hunted and put out of commission.

Detective Eli Camacho worked in a country where the most wanted drug criminal can easily "escape" a maximum security prison. He worked a land where two former governors of states bordering Texas, have been indicted in US courts for money laundering, among other charges, and who are still on the run.

Eli worked in a land where a Police Chief sought refuge with him on one of his travels within Mexico, in order to avoid assassination by a crime boss whom he had angered!

Eli worked this detail, in that environment, for over 15 years, and still managed to return over 10,000 stolen cars successfully back to the United States from Mexico.

He built networks within the law enforcement infrastructure of Mexico to effectively execute his duties as an American agent. This network included some good, honest policemen whom he built friendships with.

Detective Camacho's accounts in this series of stories that he tells in his own words, unfold a reality that takes place in a land a stone throw away from the Rio Grande, but a universe far away in terms of progress and the judicial system.

Enjoy.

A. Beresford Marcello

Introduction

After 17 years working in Mexico repatriating stolen vehicle's I started to wonder if maybe it wasn't time for me to quit. After returning thousands of stolen vehicles back to the U.S., maybe my time had come to an end. The Mexico I had known 17 years prior, was no more.

The Mexican people had a reputation of being happy, joyful, carefree, caring and welcoming people who were always friendly and willing to offer their home and help to a person in need. They lived up to the saying, "Mi casa es su casa." But sadly, things had changed. Now, doors were kept locked, people were afraid to go out, and mistrust ran rampant. I could not help but to be saddened by all that I was seeing.

Surprisingly enough, this turmoil was not only affecting strangers, in some occasions it had hit close to home. One of my wife's cousins who happens to be a successful rancher and who owns a couple of ranches in Mexico was beaten and left lying unconscious on his driveway one morning. It seemed that two individuals had been waiting for him and approached him as he was opening the gates to his driveway one morning. He was about to drive out with his truck when they approached him armed with hand guns and demanded the keys to his truck and his cell phone. He gave them the keys and said he didn't want any problem, but that wasn't enough they still beat him up. He spent a week in the hospital recovering and thankful that they had not killed him.

Then a few months later one of his son's was kidnapped from one of his cattle ranches and held for ransom for over a month until the demanded money was paid. How much he paid? I don't know for certain, but it was most likely in the thousands and in dollars not pesos.

During the same timeframe my God-daughter's husband's brother was kidnapped and a ransom was also demanded. His parents, who own a lumber and hardware store, negotiated with the kidnapper's because their demand was too high. Imagine that, having to negotiate for the life of your child? Eventually, after several tense weeks, the kidnapper's settled for less and their son was released. Even now years later the poor young man in his mid-twenties is traumatized.

All around Mexico it has become common for local buses and tourist buses alike, to be stopped on the local streets and open highways and robbed at gun point. People walking out of stores and restaurants had their vehicles carjacked by force. Sadly, the violence and crime began to envelope every aspect of people's lives.

Every morning it has become common to read in the newspaper that police have found a dead body lying on the side of a road, or in the trunk of an abandoned car, usually wrapped in a blanket. Some have even been left hanging from overpasses. Often only the headless body or simply just the head of a person is found. Sometimes with a written note or warning from the aggressors.

It seemed that people all over Mexico, including people that I knew personally had had some type of trauma over something that had happened to them or to, a relative, a friend, or a neighbor. Yet others were scared simply because of what was going on around them, wondering how safe they were and if they were going to be next. For me, at work, it wasn't much different. Dozens of my Mexican counter parts had now been killed. Some had retired others had left.

On one occasion described later in the book, an acquaintance (I actually considered him a friend) lost his life just a few hundred feet away from me. So, did I too wonder and worry that maybe I too could be a target? The answer was and is an optimistic no! I felt that I wasn't a threat to anyone, but yet at times I must confess, I did wonder. I mean, it seemed that these Mexican police officers that I had known, had breakfast or dinner with, with whom I had had meetings, a few drinks, walked around town, talked of many things, they never mentioned to me the possibility of, or feeling as they were a target.

If I felt any consolation at all it was that for the most part these officers had been killed or ambushed away from me. Most were ambushed in their police or personal cars, while walking to or from a police installations, and a few in some other circumstance. I recall a high ranking Commander once saying that these persons would never dare to attack a U.S. Law enforcement officer again. That they were aware of the problems they would bring upon themselves. Not since Kiki Camarena, had a U.S. peace officer been killed in Mexico, and this occurring to the Commander had been a big mistake.

But I was also aware and did not fool myself that there had been a couple of instances when someone innocent had been killed because they happen to be with the person who was a target at the time. Wrong place, wrong time. I often told myself that although it did happen, there weren't too many of them. It seemed to me, as if whoever it was that was doing the killing of these officers was actually trying to keep the collateral damage down. After being to the scene of a couple of these shooting and observing the scene it was amazing how the shooter or shooters were able to concentrate and keep the shots in one small circle.

These guys were good! If you ever tried shooting full automatic with a weapon, you know how hard it is to keep your hits centered close, and if you haven't, take my word for it, it's hard.

But even then there were times when I thought, these are the people I associate with in a daily bases, one could easily be at the wrong place at the wrong time, with the wrong person. I mean, I did meet with them regularly, went to lunch and so forth, even if I wasn't the direct target, I guess it could have happened. I did my best not to worry about it. But regardless, one thing I made sure of, and that was not to ride in their cars with them or give them a ride in my car if I could help it. Although at times, it just couldn't be helped.

Now, here I was, during last two years of my employment. Due to conditions in Mexico the State Department had recommended to my Agency not to allow us to travel into Mexico.

Since I was no longer allowed to travel into Mexico I had to spend my time in my office in El Paso. I have never been much of an office person. I would get done with my paperwork and help out my secretary to keep busy. I've always liked being out in the field, in the tranches. But, the recommendations of the State Department were taken very seriously, and no Americans (especially those involved in Law Enforcement) were allowed to travel into Mexico. I had been grounded.

The contact with my Mexican partners was now restricted to telephone conversations and emails. When I used to spend about 10 days out of a month in Mexico I was now relying more and more on my trusted vendors.

They continuing the work that I had started and were keeping me informed as to what was going on in Mexico. I required my vendors to come to my office once a month for a briefing and we would have brain storming sessions and discuss the things going on and the changes and adjustments that were required.

But I felt useless, I wasn't used to sitting on my butt. At the same time as I thought back on some of the things that had happened in the past and what had brought these travel restrictions in Mexico. I couldn't help but think that maybe it was a message for me to retire. I had done all I could in the last 17 years. I had received many awards and praises for the work I had done, some even called me a trail blazer. The repatriation statistics were good, relations with my counterparts were like they had never been before.

But, things had changed in other ways as well. The Mexican police had become more fearful of trying to take away stolen cars from people who might be associated with the cartels. This fear was for a good reason too. Two Federal Highway Patrol Officers had been killed in the process of stopping a stolen Hummer just outside of Juarez. In another case two State Agents had been killed over a stolen U.S. Escalade. In a separate incident, a shooting occurred in Guadalajara over some stolen vehicles. It was getting to risky for these officers, so they had stopped checking high profile vehicles at random and I really couldn't blame them.

So, in June 2009, I sadly put in my retirement papers and retired.

I haven't been back to Mexico since. I have received a few phone calls and visits from some of the people I worked with back then and they have kept me informed as to what is going on. But, every year there is less and less people that I know, it seems many have been killed, some have retired and other have left the Law Enforcement careers all together and gone to other fields of employment.

One of my good friends and ex commander is now running a restaurant here in El Paso. Another has opened a mechanic shop with his brother, and another has gone into the home alarm business and yet another one is working in Las Vegas. A very close Deputy Attorney General from Cuauhtémoc is now a federal judge. A commander from the federal Highway Patrol from Guadalajara retired and moved to Juarez and is working with a trucking company, I see him once in a while. Yet others are doing other things and I still keep in touch with some old cop friends that are still in service. We talk sometime and after all these years some of them tell me surprisingly, some facts that I was not aware of back then. But now they feel as if they can talk, they are no longer afraid nor are they obligated to anyone person or group. But even now they will say "but don't say I told you". In some occasions they have proven and confirmed some of the doubts and suspicions that I had back then.

Throughout my career I have often been referred to as an expert in Auto Theft. I've never really felt comfortable with that. I mean, to me when it comes to Auto Theft, the only expert is that guy who has been stealing cars for 20-30 years and who has never been caught. Now that's an expert. In all sincerity, I don't believe that there is such a thing as an "EXPERT" in anything. You might have someone who is more knowledgeable then others, for the mere fact that he has been doing something longer ,or researched something, or simply been around longer than others, but does that mean that he is an expert, I don't think so. There is always something to learn. Besides, an "ex" is a has-been, and a "pert" is something that drips under pressure, and I'm neither.

In retrospect, one thing I think could have gotten me into trouble, is the publicity that I was starting to get. When things started getting a little hairy many of the police and prosecutors wanting to take the pressure away from themselves or their institutions, and started to mention my name.

They started to point fingers in my direction and fault me for the job they had to do. Sometimes they referred to me as the representative of the U.S., or the American Consulate, of the Insurance Companies, of the State Police, of the FBI, or anything that would come to their mind, just as long as it would get the pressure off of themselves. Not only that, I think there was an honest confusion as to who I was and who I represented. For one, one day I would be there with an FBI agent as a partner, next time I would be there with a State Police a partner, then I would be there with a consular officer from the Consulate or Embassy office as a partner or I would be representation the Insurance Industry. So, this could have been confusing to them. Nobody like me had ever been there before doing the things that I was doing and most likely no one will do it again.

In 2012 I wrote a book about my experiences working in México, I felt as if I needed to tell someone. The book was titled "Auto Theft and the Mexican Border" I self-published my book and it went on sale in various formats.

In 2014 I met Doctor Beresford Marcello who was working for a Health Insurance company that covered my wife and me. One day as he did our yearly physical checkup we started to talk. I told him of some of the things that I went through working on Mexico and he kept asking more questions. He became aware of my book and jotted down the information.

A few months later Marcello called me and told me he had read my book and had enjoyed it tremendously, however he felt as if I had left some stuff out and he felt there was more to my story. In fact, there had been some stuff that I did leave out for various reasons. He wondered if I would be willing to sit down for a recorded interview and I agreed.

Following is that recorded interview which was done in my house one evening.

Chapter 1

Private repatriations

About six months after I had retired, I started receiving calls from Mexican Officials with whom I had previously worked with. They kept telling me that some stolen cars which were in their custody had not been picked up by their owners. They wanted me to contact the owners and let them know that their cars had been located and that they needed to pick it up.

These calls were coming from various Mexican law enforcement agencies from throughout Mexico and some were actual State Prosecutors.

Of course I informed them that I was retired and no was longer in that business, besides I no longer had access to the Police data bases and was unable to get information on owners or anything else. I recommended that they get ahold of the Police Agency which was investigating the theft or the El Paso Police Department, Texas Department of Public safety or better yet maybe NICB (National Insurance Crime Bureau). They said they already had, but apparently nothing had been done.

There were two ways that Mexican law Enforcement Agencies learned that a vehicle was stolen from the U.S.

One was when they took a vehicle into custody for any type of crime and the driver or presumed owner was unable to prove ownership or just simply failed to claim his/her vehicle afterwards and the vehicle was believed to be of U.S. origin, either because of license plates or other factors, the Mexican authority would sent a written form with the vehicle description to the nearest American Consulate (or U.S. Embassy) who in turn would check with the U.S. L.E. (Law Enforcement) agency for stolen. Sometimes this list would have multiple listings. The Consulate would reply (also in writing) if the vehicle was stolen in the U.S. or not. This would take anywhere from a few days to a few weeks.

Another way of finding out if the vehicle was stolen was (which I'm proud to say was my brain child) to contact BATIC (Border Auto Theft Information Center) which was run by the Texas Department of Public Safety in El Paso Texas. In order however to be able to call Batic the caller had to have had previous clearance to call the center and have a password. Each authorized caller had their own password.

This had been part of my job previously. As I traveled throughout Mexico meeting and training Mexican Officers. I would give training sessions to Mexican officials of various ranks (I did however prefer to concentrate on actual patrol officers or investigators) of governmental agencies. I would instruct them on what BATIC was and how to call. I would recommend those that could and those that could not call, or I would rely on one of their commanders to recommend callers. This training included how to detect stolen vehicles and how to identify those which had been altered and the U.S. - Mexico treaty procedures.

The call to BATIC (which was open 24/7) would have a reply of about two (2) minutes at the most. This was very important for those officers who needed to know right away if they had a vehicle stopped and suspected the vehicle stolen, they could not otherwise hold the vehicle and driver for too long without that stolen information ,which BATIC would supply. The officers loved the quick response and especially since they could have in in writing by means of a fax that Batic would send. BATIC would give them the case number, date of theft and location of theft (city and investigating Law Enforcement Agency). This would give the officers the needed probable cause to detain the vehicle and driver. This of course would not dismiss the Mexican officer from later on sending the information to the AC (American Consulate) as required by the U.S/Mexico treaty.

The standard procedure would then require that the U.S. Law Enforcement Agency which had been notified ether by the American Consulate or BATIC of the stolen vehicle location and seizure, to then inform the owner.

Before I started working Mexico, with the exception of the treaty process, there was no other procedure except for what had been developed on a local and personal nature. Even the treaty process was unknown to many Mexican and some U.S. L.E. agencies. Many of the Mexican Law Enforcement Agencies and some individual officers had made contact with individual U.S. Law Enforcement Officers, Border Patrol, local Police or Sheriff Departments and even the FBI. This personal contact would enable Mexican officers to have an established means of exchanging information.

The lengthy means of going through the treaty process was not preferable by Mexican officers (or anyone else).

After I started working, I saw this and I heard complaints from Mexican officers as I did my travels and tours throughout

Mexico. Gradually once BATIC was established, more and more, Mexican authorizes staring using my sources. It got to the point where it was not only used for stolen vehicles, but other information as well, including wanted individuals from the U.S.

The calls that I was now receiving, after retirement, were because one of these two previously mentioned procedures had already taken place. The vehicle was in custody, time had gone by and apparently the car owner had not shown up to claim the stolen U.S.Vehicle.

With the experience that I had obtain I knew that one of 5 things had now occurred.

1. The owner was notified and he rushed from the United States to Mexico to claim his vehicle. Once there he found out he didn't have the proper paperwork to claim the vehicle. The owner thought that it would be sufficient to show the vehicle's title, but it was not. Some Mexican agencies actually required the full U.S./Mexico treaty process. In occasions the owner became frustrated after spending days and a good amount of money and went back home to complain to the U.S. Law Enforcement Agency he/she reported the vehicle stolen to originally.

2. The owner arrived to claim his/her vehicle and even if he/she had the proper paperwork was still not given his vehicle. This was because in Mexico when a vehicle is involved in a crime it becomes evidence and won't be released until no longer needed by the courts. This could take weeks, months, or sometimes years. (

although there is a way, most owners would not know and would not be informed)

3. The vehicle was no place to be found when the owner arrived. This could be because the vehicle had actually been recovered in another city, which was dependent on the authorities from where the call originated from. Or it was being used by the Mexican Authority, or the authorities were making it difficult for the owner, wanting and waiting for a reward to be offered.

4. The vehicle was a total loss, either stripped or wrecked. Whenever possible I would caution the owner of taking the word of the Mexican Official he spoke with in regards to the vehicle condition. Sometimes over the phone, the person talking, without actually knowing, would say that the vehicle was in good condition when it was not. And in some cases they would tell you the reverse that it was a total loss, when it was not. That was because they wanted to keep it, or in fact didn't know.

5. Or the owner was notified but he/she no longer owned the vehicle, the insurance had paid them off and they were no longer interested. In some cases the insurance was never notified and they were unaware of the recovery. Or it was an older car, the owner had already replaced it and was no longer interested in investing money to bring the old vehicle back to the U.S. The same thing was true of many insurance companies. Usually a vehicle 5 years old or older would not be repatriated, they would (or already had) written it off.

And of course there were always those cases in which the owners had no insurance and due to financial reasons could not afford to travel into Mexico and make the necessary expenses to recover their vehicle. There were also some who had no knowledge of Mexico and who were afraid to travel into Mexico and who needed someone to help them or otherwise they preferred to lose the vehicle. And then there was one more. The owner was deceased, or moved with no forwarding address and he couldn't be located.

And then of course there was the case where the owner (usually the insurance company) did NOT want the vehicle back.

This was due to the fact the driver (and passengers in some cases) had been attacked and killed while using the vehicle and there was blood, body fluids, brain matter, and bone fragments splattered all over inside the vehicle. These elements had quickly soaked into the fibers of the carpet, seats and other overhead material cover. After days of the vehicle sitting in the hot Mexican sun with the car doors closed, it was not a pleasant sight nor smell. In other cases some of these vehicles had been used to place wrapped bodies of individuals who had been previously executed. They were wrapped in blankets and put in the trunk of the vehicle which was then abandoned. Not until someone could not stand the smell and called police was it detected that there was a body inside. It was very hard to remove the smell.

So, for the most part I did nothing, after telling the Mexican officials that I was retired.

However in 2009 (around December). I had a call from a car owner from Colorado. It seemed that one of the Mexican Officers in Zacatecas who knew me, had given him my phone number. This man owned a small business and had a small fleet of trucks. One of his company trucks which had been stolen had now been found in Zacatecas. He was self-insured and was unable to travel to Mexico to claim his truck and had failed to find someone who would help him. He had been told by one of the Mexican officers that I might be able to help. I really didn't want to, but he kept on insisting and offered to pay me. I was finally convinced by this man and I told him that I would look into it.

I made a few phone calls and learned that vehicle was drivable condition and a quick release could be obtained. No one had been taken into custody. It was the State Police who had it and it was being kept at their headquarters. I contacted a person I knew in Zacatecas that could help me with the foot work and I accepted the assignment. The owner then faxed me the required paperwork. My contact and I got the vehicle back for the owner in a couple of weeks. He, needless to say was very pleased as the vehicle was in very good condition.

My contact in Zacatecas liked the money and asked me to continue the repatriation of these stolen vehicles that he was willing to help me, that there were some vehicles that were being left behind.

I thought about it for about two seconds, then figured, why not? And I started to repatriate vehicles form Mexico for those car owners that needed my help.

Eventfully spreading the word throughout Mexico I started getting more and more helpers as I went along. I obtained a

Texas Private Investigators license. I got the Texas Department of Motor vehicles registration data base. Made business arrangements with U.S. and Mexico towing companies and for the next two years helped repatriate stolen vehicles from Mexico.

After two years I decided to again call it quits. I realized how difficult it was becoming to deal with certain people. As I became more successful I started to encounter jealousies, suspicions, and greed, more then I was willing to deal with. And what saddened me more than anything was that some of it came from U.S. Law Enforcement Agencies.

I worked as a Private Investigator for few more months then went into full retirement. And besides I had found a new hobby (writing) which was taking more of my time.

Calls continued, but I ignored them till finally they stopped.

Chapter 2

Becoming a Peace Officer

ABM = A. Beresford Marcello
EC= Elias Camacho

ABM: Ok this is the first track taping with Mr. Elias Camacho, former detective and El Paso police officer. Mr. Camacho, tell us what led you to the police force and then subsequently to become a detective, and then ultimately to the car theft department?

EC: You know Al, I'm a strong believer in destiny. Originally after leaving the Navy I wanted to do something that would be good for my community and at the same time earn me a good living. Unfortunately I didn't have much of an education. I dropped out of school four months into the 10th grade to join the Navy. Since I was only 16 I had to wait 6 months till I turned 17. It was not until I was in the Navy that I received my GED.

I had received a lot of training and had attended various firefighting schools as a Navy Seaman. It was something I really aspired to. Once I was discharged (I got an early discharge) and came back home I had to report to the Naval reserve. My Ship was going back to Vietnam and since I had less the six months, they transferred me over to the reserve.

During that time I took the City Fireman test. But to my surprise and to the surprise of many, I failed the fire fighter entrance exam by two points.

I couldn't believe it when I received the letter from the City of El Paso giving me my score. As I mentioned before, when I took the test, I was in the Navy reserve and my commanding officer happened to be the city personnel director. When he found out that I had not passed the exam, he too couldn't believe it. I remember him holding my service record and saying: "You've been a fireman in the Navy!" "You must have had a bad day." "I'm talking to the fire chief about you and I want you to come to my office next week".

The following week I presented myself at his office and as luck would have it, I was informed he was out of the office. While there, I happened to see a bulletin board with an announcement from the Police Department stating they were hiring. Something just moved me to apply, and here I am now, thirty-nine years later and retired from the Police Department.

On a few occasions while in the Navy I had served as shore patrol and I must admit it gave me a good feeling. So the thought of being in law enforcement wasn't entirely new to me; but in all honesty, I thought police work was for a special type of person. I thought that people in law enforcement had a different outlook than my own.

But having failed the fireman tests really made woke me up and made me feel challenged. I knew I had to take the police test even if it was out of disappointment, despair and anger.

Despite of all my previous experiences, I really didn't have any idea of what to expect. I had no idea what it took to be a policeman or how a police department operated. It wasn't until I was accepted into the Police Academy that I realized all the elements that originate a police officer. It wasn't as simply as I had thought, but neither was it so impossible.

After graduating from the police academy I was assigned to patrol division, just like any other new officer was at the time. As a new officer patrolling, I did everything. I mean my duties were not categorized like nowadays. I could be attending to a traffic accident in one moment and then a family dispute, burglary or a homicide next. I would handle different type of calls. I was a true Jack of all trades. As it was customary at the time.

As demanding as this was, it gave me very good introduction into the investigation of all types of criminal activities. It's important to highlight that in many of the theft and robbery crimes that I investigated, there was always a common factor. Most of the time there was a car involved in the criminal activity. Besides putting out an alert on a perpetrator, a description of a vehicle was always reported.

I learned that for the most part people use transportation (a car or a truck) to commit the crime and then again to flee from the crime scene.

Many times the vehicle used was also previously stolen or stolen during the commission of the crime. While on duty, my team always seemed to be looking, not only for an individual who was wanted, but for a car that was being driven by said individual.

So after completing five years in patrol I became eligible and met all qualifications to take the exam to become a detective. I liked the idea of going into the auto theft division. I felt that was easy, I mean how hard is it to find a stolen car? After I passed the test I was promoted to detective. I requested to work in the auto theft division, and I was lucky enough to get it, which was unusual, as usually a new detective would simply be assigned to where ever they were needed.

I lasted 10 years working in the auto theft division and obtained a vast amount of experience dealing with stolen cars. Aside from my hands-on experience I also attended yearly advanced auto theft trainings and seminars.

Living in a border city such as the El Paso/Juarez corridor one can't help but notice that most stolen cars were never or seldom ever found. They simply seem to disappear! In the event that car thieves were captured, we noticed a similar pattern. They were most often young kids who not only stole the vehicle, but were used to deliver the stolen vehicles to someone in Mexico. It was not as if the stolen car was for their own use.

Most often these juveniles had ties to Mexico. In some cases they were illegally in the U.S. and in other cases they were not. We had to be careful because all of them, especially if they had a visa, would always give us false information. They did this to hide their true identity and keep from losing their immigration visa. They gave us false names, false date of births and false addresses.

I also learned that many of these thieves were specialists on what they were stealing. They were experts at stealing a specific type of vehicle. It took some of the young perpetrators less than 10 seconds to break into a car or truck. Catching them was difficult and we mostly caught them while we were on stakeouts. We would often use decoys or bait vehicles.

To help the cause, on some occasions we even went to the extreme and conducted our own covert operations. I say extreme, because it entailed going to Mexico outside of our jurisdiction to try to locate and identify those who were part of the scheme. We were actually working in another Country. These covert operation allowed us to pretend to be normal people who were shopping or whatever and we tried to blend in.

For obvious reasons we never took any of our police I.D. with us. Fortunately we were successful in locating some of these stolen cars and trucks. Most of our discoveries took place early in the morning around 5 or 6 o'clock after long hours of night work. We often found stolen vehicles in high traffic places such as hotels and store parking lots that were used as drop off points.

On one occasion, we actually stole back a vehicle. I remember we were staking it out until eventually we saw a person come out of one of the hotel rooms to put some stuff in the trunk of the stolen vehicle. As carefully as possible, while this person went back to his room, we jumped into the car and using a previously obtained key started the car and drove off. We then drove to the American Consulate to hide and search the car in a safer place. We found personal belongings and an identification badge and credentials belonging to a Mexican Federal Police officer.

I truly enjoyed going to Mexico and working undercover. At times we worked with some of our trustworthy Mexican counter-parts. It was really such a rush knowing that what I was doing was dangerous. I liked it.

That is what led me into becoming a specialists in auto

theft and eventually becoming more specifically qualified dealing with Mexico.

Not only had I become good at the identification of stolen cars, but I also became good at knowing the techniques and methods used when stealing vehicles and heavy equipment. As time went on I also started doing training sessions and mentoring other law enforcement officers.

I would spend a lot of time at the abandoned vehicles impound yard training myself looking for confidential identification numbers on these cars and noticing certain manufactory patterns.

When the new cars came out I would visit the local car dealers to familiarize myself with the new VIN plates and checking for any changes.

Many things I kept to myself and some I would share with my coworkers.

Chapter 3

Working in Mexico

A BM: *Ok Mr. Camacho so you served as an El Paso Police Officer and then you went on to become a Texas Ranger and Commissioned Agent for an agency that took you into Mexico investigating stolen cars, tell us about that, car theft?

EC: Yes, during my years as an auto theft detective I had been able establish myself as pretty knowledgeable on the subject. And due to my expertise in auto theft combined with my experience working in Mexico, in 1992 I was offered a position with a national agency that was a semi quasi-law enforcement agency that not only worked in Mexico, but actually worked globally.

The offer specifically called for working in Mexico. Along with the offer as a special agent, came a commission from the Texas Department of Public Safety (TDPS) as a Special Texas Ranger. This was to better enable me to do my job as I would be able to communicate and interchange information with other law enforcement personnel. This commission would also allow me to have access to police computers and data bases.

I retired from the El Paso Police Department to work with this new agency in July 1992.

At first I was only expected to work in Juarez Chihuahua

Mexico, right across the border from El Paso. That area I had worked as a liaison with the El Paso Police Department and was very well familiar with it and the Mexican Agencies. Gradually as I became more successful in my area of responsibility my area was increased to include the whole Mexican State of Chihuahua, which borders with Texas.

This new role banned me from carrying a firearm in Mexico. Carrying a weapon in Mexico was a very serious offense. It was not easy to let go of my firearm. Especially crossing the border because at one point, Chihuahua was known as the murder capital of the world having more murders per capita than any other city. It's still a dangerous place, but not as dangerous as before.

I worked with this agency for 17 years and by the time I retired from this agency, I was not only working the Mexican State of Chihuahua but also the Mexican States of Durango, Zacatecas, Aguascalientes, Jalisco, Colima, and Nayarit. The last couple of years of employment I was also working the states of Tamaulipas, San Luis Potosi, Nuevo Leon, and Coahuila. All these are located on the Lower Valley part of Texas. I zigzagged this area in my company car meeting Mexican authorities from all levels.

Furthermore, I was also sent to assignments in El Salvador, Dominican Republic, and Panama.

Badges worn by S/A Elias Camacho

In the name and by the authority of

The State  of Texas

Be it known that

_____ ELIAS CAMACHO _____

of the City of _____ El Paso _____ , _____ El Paso _____ *County, Texas, having fulfilled the requirements of law and having been approved by the Public Safety Commission of the State of Texas, is appointed and commissioned as a*

Special Texas Ranger

and is hereby commissioned as a law enforcement officer as authorized by Section 411.024, Government Code, V.T.C.A., and is entitled to all the rights, privileges, and emoluments appertaining to said appointment.

In testimony whereof, *I have, with the approval of the Public Safety Commission of the State of Texas, hereunto signed my name and caused the seal of the Department of Public Safety, of the State of Texas, to be affixed at the City of Austin, this the* _____ 1st *day of* _____ January _____ *A.D., 20* _ 05

DIRECTOR, DEPARTMENT OF PUBLIC SAFETY

FOR THE PUBLIC SAFETY COMMISSION

Chapter 4

Crime in Mexico

A BM: *Mexico is known as an unsafe place in general. So the next question to Mr. Camacho is to talk about crime in Mexico, in the border really for the past decade and how it has affected the common person and how law enforcement has addressed it?

EC: When it comes to common people in the U.S. side of the border, crime committed in Mexico, for the most part, don't affect them at all. Especially if you don't live in the border. However, car theft greatly affects them economically. For example, they often have higher auto insurance premiums but most importantly, they experience great psychological effects, especially if involved and during a carjacking.

A victim of crime typically experiences feelings of fear and insecurity. The majority of people living in the U.S. don't visit Mexico anymore even if they have relatives living on the other side of the border. Before the recent outburst in violence, people used to go across the river for entertainment, shopping and to visit relatives. I knew many people who went regularly for dentists visits; however, that has really changed in the last decade._

When it comes to the Mexican National who lives in

Mexico, they are definitely affected. We can imagine the impact being at a more personal level.

But you know, it's funny that you ask that question, as far as crime in general in Mexico, I don't think anybody really knows or has the statistics of how much crime really happens in Mexico. People in Mexico generally don't report crime. When people see a crime being committed, they will walk the other way or simply look away. They don't want to become involved, they are afraid.

For the most part this is something that doesn't happen in the U.S. The U.S. police officer solves many of its crimes because citizens call in with information, people get involved. The U.S. citizen has no fear of being identified as the person that called. Because their information and identity is kept secret, not so in Mexico. Although it could also be true in Mexico that identities can be kept secret, people don't trust the law enforcement system regardless of the type of crime that was committed. Very often citizens feel that their police officers don't have the professionalism needed to do a good job nor a truly interest in solving the crime. In most cases, the police could even be suspected of being part of the criminal enterprise. They don't believe the law enforcement system will do anything for them.

Who can trust officers that most likely are involved in the crime directly or indirectly? So, what is the sense of reporting a crime?

Due to such circumstances, I really don't think anyone really knows how much crime actually occurs in Mexico; therefore, politicians use this to their advantage. The news media often try to show a different picture and tell things differently.

They paint a different picture than what's really occurring. The effects are usually minimized or totally exaggerated by media. We, in the U.S. often don't hear about it. For example, take the dozens and dozens of young girls who have disappeared in Ciudad Juarez, Chihuahua in the past years. Those cases have never been solved. Dozens of decayed bodies of young girls have been found out in the desert area and no one has been arrested. People in the U.S. would never stand for something like this, they would put so much pressure on the law enforcement agencies and politicians that heads would be rolling.

Aside from the killing of young women in Mexico, the violence brought by the cartel wars has been overwhelming for everyone. The lack of government interaction has made it all much worse.

I think Mexico would not have such a high rate of crime if it was not for the blanket of corruption that exist within its communities and culture as a whole.

Many of the law enforcement personnel and sometimes whole agencies are bought off by cartels. Due to the drug war their lives are in danger so they would rather become part of the problem by keeping silent. It is not uncommon for a police officer of any rank to be given a choice, either you help or you're dead. We often hear the phrase of "Plata o Plomo" (silver or lead) this is very, very true. A police officer in Mexico can't be neutral, he has to take sides.

For the common citizen, who has means, its common practice is to hire a law enforcement officer to do something about the crime that has been committed against them, without making an official complain. For example, I saw many

ELIAS CAMACHO

reward signs up at the police offices in Mexico where citizens were offering rewards to police officers for finding a stolen car or a missing person, or whatever. Not until a reward is offered will many officers go out of their way to solve cases because now, it's worth it for them. For the most part people in Mexico don't do anything about it because they don't have the money to pay a reward. I have noticed that Mexican citizens have normalized crime as something that ought to happen and can only hope the effects are minimal.

I also say that the common person, the Mexican citizen or tourist is to a certain extent guilty for the corruption in Mexico. Knowingly or unknowingly the common person contributes to it. Take for example a simple case involving a traffic ticket where a person gets stopped for a violation and they offer to pay the officer a bribe. They give him 10 bucks or even less and the officer accepts and withdraws. The same is true when a U.S. citizen pays a Mexican customs officer to allow them to bring something illegal into Mexico, or when a drug dealer pays off a police officer to look the other way. Sadly, crime is so embedded into the culture.

We can't deny that there are great benefits for those who are somehow part of and involved with the drug cartels.

I support this statement by sharing with you the events that occurred at a dinner ceremony I attended where I was actually being recognized and honored for my work. This ceremony took place one evening back in 2002 in Cuauhtémoc Chihuahua. After dinner and a few drinks the conversations became pretty candid among the attendees which numbered about 15. Among them was the area prosecutor, high ranking police officers and some business people. 80% of them said that the economy in Cuauhtémoc is better with the cartels than without them. As long as the cartels are not at war with each other, the city will prosper and benefit in many ways. When the cartels are running smoothly there is employment for hundreds of people. Citizens are hired for the growing, cultivating, processing and shipping of the drugs. Many young men get jobs as laborers, guards, drivers, packers, and so forth. They all get paid good money. They buy food, clothing, TVs, cars, and many other things because they have money. The stores in Cuauhtémoc are enjoying good sales and new stores are opening up. Crime is down and the town prospers.

Something their own government does not do for them. When the question of morality and decency came up, they reply that the drugs are going to the U.S., to the addicted "gringos." These Gringos will get the drugs from somewhere, so why not from Mexico.

As long as their own people are not using the drugs, and when they are employed they usually don't, then who cares! People need jobs and stability and this is something they get when the cartels are doing well. Of course, I for the most part, reserved my opinions at that time. I did more listening than talking. I just simply listened to people speak and comment and when asked what I thought, I would neither agree nor disagree, and either say "I don't know" and when pressured would slightly favor their opinions, after all, it did make sense.

It was very interesting to hear what people in Mexico really thought.

But you know, corruption has not discriminated against the U.S. either. As a Commander once said "You guys are not white pigeons" meaning we are also blemished. We carry our own corruption and we haven't been able to stop it. All though it is true that maybe it's not as open as it is in Mexico, does that make it acceptable? Does that make it alright?

You asked me to comment on what U.S. Law enforcement is doing. There is not much it can do, at least not on Mexican soil. Maybe obtain intelligence, and keep abreast as to who is who and who is doing what, and that's about it. Our government keeps putting money into Mexico as if it's going to solve the problem, but I don't think it will.

S/A Elias Camacho (3rd from L) with Mexican State Police.

Chapter 5

How big is the Auto Theft Problem?

A BM: *You mentioned earlier that just about every crime that's committed involves a vehicle. That brings us to car theft on the border, tell us how big of a problem that is, how big of an industry that is, and how that affects the average American person?

EC: You know the auto theft situation along the border is a lucrative multi-billion dollar business. But it's not restricted to the border. New York and other cities are not in the border and have a sufficient auto theft problem as well. Thousands and thousands of cars are stolen every year and one would think it would be more prominent along the border because it's close proximity to Mexico. But, that's not necessarily the case. However, having said that, Mexico is one of the biggest consumers of stolen U.S. vehicles for various reasons. And because of this, it also invites fraud which is not often addressed.

Many of these stolen vehicles that do make it into Mexico are used in crimes and some for resale, either whole or in parts. There is a big demand for auto parts, so chop shops are very common. You might not believe this, but you can get more money for a car in parts then you can whole. The drug cartels use a large fleet of stolen vehicles as well to transport drugs, among other things.

In about 75% of the cases in which an executed person is found inside a vehicle, 95% of the time that vehicle is a stolen vehicles. These statistics of course are my own statistics, there is no formal study done that I know of. I just go by recalling certain cases. Also, a very large amount of individuals who were executed out in the open and left lying on the streets had a job that was related to vehicles industry. They either were in the business of importing (many of them stolen) cars, fixed cars, had junk yards, and so on.

What does this tell you? Stolen cars are in the center of most of the criminal activity. Many stolen cars are traded for drugs and the ever need for transportation needs from the cartels are supplied through stolen vehicle channels.

Cartels also utilize vehicles not only to transport drugs into the United States, but also to transport the drugs down from the growing fields in the mountains of Mexico. For example, large F250 pick-up truck and diesel 4x4 trucks are used up in the mountains and rough terrains to bring down the freshly cut product down to the cities where they are processed, packed and so forth.

There are also those luxury type cars that are being driven by drug lords, their families, girlfriend, and maybe even their maids. I'm not saying that everyone driving a stolen vehicle is aware that the vehicle is stolen. There are cases in which the person has no knowledge of this.

I recall a case that happen during one of my visits to El Salvador. It involved the media informing the public that some

"Americans" were in town looking for stolen cars. That's not exactly how they said it, and there was several misleading details, but nonetheless a sweep did take place conducted by the Salvadorian National Police. Within the Salvadorians that had stolen cars was a local priest. Of course the priest did not steal it, it was given to him by a parishioner.

These types of activities have been going on for a long time and it's something that for the most part, the normal citizens is not aware of. It's also not considered news worthy for local media. Media channels often seek news that includes blood, guts and all that is gory! Well, I've got news for them, there is plenty of violence involved in the stealing of cars. And not only in Mexico but in the U.S. as well.

It isn't uncommon for law enforcement in the U.S. to have violent sometimes deadly encounters during traffic stops when unbeknownst to them they are stopping a stolen car.

Referencing to the car theft industry, it's a vicious cycle. Victims of a stolen car call the insurance company to report their car stolen. The insurance company pays them off. And often much less than what the car is worth. Since victims figure there's not much they can do, they move on to purchasing a new vehicle, usually having to fiancé all or part. Business wise, the thief has a car, the car dealer sells a car, and the bank lends money on a car, see what is occurring here? This occurs over and over again.

As I mentioned before, this opens a new window of opportunity to another type of crime, fraud. Fraud is responsible for millions of false claims adding up to millions and millions of dollars lost in the insurance industry. Anyway, victims purchase a new vehicle, the Insurance Company raises its rates, and all the owner can do is hope and wait that they are not re-victimize.

The industry of stolen cars is a very lucrative business. It involves extremely powerful people. I don't think it's something that we will see an end to anytime soon. 100 years ago it was cattle and horses that were stolen and the thieves were hung if caught. That didn't stop them. So, today it's cars and trucks. I really can't foresee anything that will curtail it.

The common person may think that it's only Mexico that's consuming our stolen cars but they are wrong because these cars are going to other places around the world as well. Without knowing it, the United States has become a world-wide distributor of stolen vehicles.

One thing that is happening in our seaports may it be in California and Florida or our eastern ports, is that many stolen vehicles are leaving our country in containers on ships. And not only from the United States, but from Mexican seaports as well.

Many of the stolen cars from the U.S leave the country almost immediately after they are stolen. Often times they are altered to the point that they can't be identified. Should a Police Officer happen to stop one of these altered stolen cars it is very difficult for him to identify the car due to its alterations. Officers need specific expertise to be able to check for tell tail signs. The averaged Police officer will not be successful. I've seen some thieves do such a good a job that it would envy the manufactures.

Mexican State Police looking for marijuana fields

Chapter 6
Negotiations & Network

A BM: *So Mr. Camacho you worked with a network of law enforcement and that helped you pioneer in the fighting the crime of car theft, such that it resulted in you returning well over ten thousand cars back to the United States from Mexico. Talk a little bit about that network that you created and how you were so successful in negotiating that network to return over ten thousand cars to the United States.

EC: Yeah, I guess I can start by sharing how I would create my contacts. One of the things that assisted me in this process was the fact that I was providing training in Mexico and other countries. This in its self was a door opener because not only were they receiving well needed training but it was coming from the U.S. which they respected greatly. I was training Mexican law enforcement officers in the detection of stolen cars and it was being recommended by the Embassy and Consulates, or in cases they would request training from the Embassy or Consulates and we would be recommended. For one thing with the exception of the FBI other L.E. agencies don't work in Mexico or other foreign countries. This way they knew it was a bonafide, approved and qualified agency that was doing the training, and was being done by a non for profit as well. And it would cost them nothing. (There were at the time and maybe still is, private companies doing training in Mexico for a fee) So, this is the way I got my foot inside the door.

However, I never called it training. I never told them that I was going to go over there and *teach* them anything. I did not want to insult them. I didn't want them to think of me as a "big super American auto theft detective" I did not want them to feel that I was going to teach them because they did not know better, that they were ignorant. I took their pride into consideration.

These guys had pride and they didn't want anybody, especially somebody from the U.S. to come over and teach them anything. I mean that's an insult nobody wants, especially Mexican law enforcement officers. For the most part they felt they had been doing a good job with what they had for years and they didn't want the Gringos to come and teach them. Like anybody else they had their pride. The training was usually requested by politicians or higher up's in certain agencies so that they could get credit and show the people that they were becoming professionals.

Many of the lower level rank and file felt that we Americans were arrogant, know it all, and used our money and power to get others to do what we wanted and in the process, knowingly or not, we belittle people. (Many told me this after they got to trust me) Many Mexicans don't see us in a very good light. I had to be careful with that. How is that saying? "You get more flies with sugar than you do with vinegar?"

Many of them had been in law enforcement for years and they had accomplish wonders in their investigations. We must not underestimate them.

They got things done with little or no technical tools or know how, just plain common sense. I give them credit for that. I would always tell them that I was going to visit them and tell them some of my experiences and interchange ideas so hopefully I could learn from them as well, that we could learn from each other. I would say things like" this is the way WE do it, you might do it different, let's compare".

I often highlight cases that they had solved. I would tell them that we in the United States are experts in losing cars, but that they are the experts in finding them. This always got a good laugh.

During these training sessions I would make friends and I always tried to get them involved by asking for their point of view, their opinions, and any other feedback they wanted to share with me. I always tried to listened more and talk less, because I found that it made them curious about what I had to say. I wanted them to be the ones wanting my input and I would gladly give it to them once they asked. This led to many friendships. Being honest and sincere was always my goal.

It was not unusual that after training session we would go down to a local watering hole and have a beer or two. It is amazing how much they would share with me and how it would get us closer. They would talk about their organizations, how they felt, why they took certain actions, why they did somethings or why they did not and their short comings.

Some of them admitted outright how much help they needed and how willing they were in the interchange of ideas and information.

They were also very interested on how police worked in

the U.S. and what drove them. Many of them, all they knew was what they saw on TV and felt a great respect of the highly trained, well-disciplined US officers. I made funny jokes a couple of times that American Police could solve any crime in 30 minutes, commercials included. Once they trusted you, there was nothing they wouldn't tell you. I got so much intelligence this way you wouldn't believe.

I don't mean to insult anyone, but rest assure that I was the first person that reported that "La Lina" cartel organization had been formed and was headquartered in Villa Humada and that the leader was an ex-cop. I saw the birth of that cartel organization and knew some of its founders.

Now, were there some dirty cops that were perhaps attempting to get intelligence from me? I wouldn't doubt it! I was very careful on what I said. I always remembered an old detective movie where the detective acted kind of dumb and never knew anything. Some of you might remember the old TV series from the 70's, with Peter Faulk who played the character Colombo. Boy, that Colombo, he was my hero. Partnering up with Mexican officers and U.S. officers was my strategy. We would hang out together whenever possible.

One thing that was very common with all the Mexican agencies I worked with regardless if they were Municipal, State or Federal, was them wondering why they could not get monetary rewards for recovering stolen vehicles. They would tell me of how the Mexican insurance companies would always give them a percentage of the value of the car whenever they found a stolen Mexican car. If the Mexican insurance companies could do it, why couldn't the U.S. Insurance companies do the same? This they claimed was a motivator. It was widely known by some that on occasions some people would also go over from the U.S. insurance companies and offer money, so why didn't I? It was difficult to find a worthy response since it's customary in Mexico to give a gratuity to the individual officer as a job well done.

Not only that, but there were some U.S. Law Enforcement personnel who would often encourage American citizens to offer a reward. If Mexican citizens receive a call from an officer stating that they have found their car, they would give the officer a gratuity. Why not all of the American car owners? They felt there was nothing wrong with that.

Yet I worked under different rules and employment conditions I explained.

We would not and could not pay anybody. They wondered why the United States would compensate citizens through crime stoppers, what's the difference they would say, why could they not be compensated.

Knowing how much they admired the U.S. Police Officers I would tell them that the only way to become an actual professional in our chosen field of Law Enforcement and if we wanted to be respected by our citizens, as well as peers , the first thing we needed to do was forget about gratuities. I would appeal to their professionalism, devotion to family and country, and whatever I could at the moment to convince them that asking for money was not part of the job, nor was it right.

Some would agree and others would simply frown, but I knew they would not act on it and I left it up to the conscious of each individual. Their points was well taken, and to further make their point a few would say "we are risking our lives every time we find one of these cars, and they aren't even stolen in Mexico and you guys can't compensate us?"

You can't imagine how many times I was taken back to this topic throughout my career in Mexico and how lengthy our discussions were and how often we didn't get anywhere and only agreed to disagree. .

As new officers came onboard, this was always on their mind. The same questions and I would simply reply, "I see you, I'm with you, however", and I would make my pitch. This pattern and habit had been established in Mexico many years before I started coming over, which I realized was difficult for them to break away from. But, there was really nothing more I could do, except reach those that I could. I just did my best and looked for ways to help them. I won some over, others I did not.

When vehicles were recovered in Mexico, they had to be taken into custody and had to go into impound yards whenever they were available. I say whenever they were available because in some smaller cities, rural areas and towns there were no storage facilities and these vehicles would simply be parked in front of the Police Station ,which in many cases were confiscated homes. They were held there until the owner came to claim them and then transported back to the U.S.

But before this could be done, a lengthy process of paperwork took place. Documents had to be submitted, notarized, certified copies, apostils and power of attorney's created. A lengthy and time consuming process. Finally after weeks or months the vehicle was released to be taken back to U.S. It was picked up from wherever it was being held.

Originally when I first started I found it more economically beneficial (and rewarding to the Mexican Officers) if I hired the Mexican Police Officers that located these vehicle as the drivers to transport these vehicles to the international boundary. Most of the vehicles were in fairly good drivable and running condition. And being that they knew they would drive it back to the U.S. they would keep from stripping off parts. Hiring these same officers that seized the stolen car was a good way to pay them for their work.

They were happy, but I couldn't always hire them for various reasons and after some time I had to hire others and eventually I started using tow trucks. There's two main reasons why I had to do that.

One, was the possible liability if an accident was to have occurred, and there was still another more compelling reason, let me explain.

One time we recovered a stolen Suburban in Parral Chihuahua. Two Texas State troopers, Sgt. Fernando Aguilar and Sgt. Manny Lozano were with me on this trip. Oscar, one of my vendors had been hired to drive the vehicle back to Chihuahua City. After obtaining the release and taking the vehicle out of the impound yard, we stopped to fill up the gas tank on the recovered stolen Suburban. We followed Oscar as he drove out of Parral unto the road that lead to Chihuahua. We following him (the Sergeants and I were in my vehicle) a short distance behind. I was driving a Cherokee at the time. Anyway, as we drove out of the city and as we neared a cross roads we noticed a Dodge Durango with real dark tinted windows pass us and get between Oscar and us. The Durango sped up and came abreast with Oscar who opened the window after being motioned to do so by the passenger in the Durango. We then observed Oscar pull off the road into the dirt portion of a parking lot of a roadside restaurant. The Durango followed close behind Oscar. We thought that maybe it was a friend of Oscar who had flagged him down, but we were not sure.

Oscar stopped and the Durango stopped alongside of him. Two Mexican cowboy type individuals got out from the Durango and so did Oscar. The Durango driver and passengers who got out were dressed and looked like drug dealers or maybe even cops. In some cases there wasn't much difference in their appearance. The guys driving the Durango walked towards Oscar and we then observed the two individuals and Oscar talking standing between both vehicles. While doing so, after a couple of minutes, Oscar turned and pointed towards us. We had parked about 30 yards or so behind them. Fernie, Manny and I kept wondering what it could be, why was Oscar pointing at us. I then started to get an uneasy feeling, like when your gut tells you something is not right. I started thinking, since we are unarmed and if something were to go down, I would use my car as a weapon. I would speed up and run them over.

All this time neither one of us said anything, we just kept looking towards Oscar and observing the body language. After a while the cowboy looking driver got back into their Durango followed by the passenger who looked back at us as he did. As they were getting into their Durango they both turned and looked at us one last time. They then sped off and we pulled up to Oscar to find out what had happened.

Oscar told us that those were the guys who had possession of the stolen Suburban and who had been driving it when it was taken away from them by the Mexican State Police. They claimed ownership when it was taken from them but the Mexican State Police did not release it back to them due to the fact it was reported stolen in the U.S. They wanted to know who Oscar was and why he was driving the Suburban. Oscar told them that he was taking it back to the U.S. and that he was working for us, that we were U.S. State Police officers. Oscar said that after he said that, they drove off. Oscar said that at first they were very aggressive and demanding, but once he told them we were parked behind him and who we were, they simply said okay and left. Oscar asked us if we had noticed that they were armed and of course we never noticed it. Apparently they were drug dealers.

There was another situation in which a Durango was involved. After obtaining its release we filled up the gas tank to drive it back to the U.S., but it kept running out of gas about every 50 miles or so.

We couldn't figure it out why it kept doing that, the fuel gage showed full. Once back in the U.S. we checked it at U.S. Customs, after dropping the gasoline tank we found it was full of marihuana bricks. Enough gas would fit only to drive a short distance. It was then that I decided it was best to tow these vehicles.

I didn't want to take a change of being challenged by the thieves or drug dealers who had been using these vehicles. The recoveries were now done by wrecker if close to the border or by trucking companies if it was a long distance, the vehicles stored inside semi-truck covered trailers.

I came to learn a lot about the Mexican culture when it came to dealing with certain business people. So much that I knew that I was being over charged, I was being charged more than the normal customer would be. This included the storage yards, towing and trucking companies.

It was a common practice that American citizens would always be over charged. They figured the Americans had a lot of money and could afford it. I knew this, but by the same token, I was doing business with a legal company that was giving me receipts, there was not much I could do about it. I couldn't tell them how to run their business, how much to charge nor could I go to their competitor, since there was no one else in some cases. If I complained, (which I did sometimes) it did no good, only delayed the process. And besides their charges and their services weren't really regulated, they could charge whatever they wanted. I was fully aware and realize that I too had turned the other way and ignored what was really happening. What was really happening was that the towing company was overcharging me to a certain extent because part of the over charged money went back to the officer that had seized the stolen vehicle.

If I didn't pay them (bribe), they would find another way to get it. Other arrangements had been done. They had their thing going, I wasn't fooled, and I think they knew that I knew, but everyone was happy. Was it wise to report it? I don't think so, it would have gotten me no place except to make enemies and maybe even stop the repatriation of the vehicles. And besides, even with the overcharge, it was still acceptable compared to the U.S. cost of recovery. I personally didn't see anything wrong with it.

I wish I could have given the guy $50 or $100 bucks, it was worth it, and it was worth it if you knew the type of pay these officers made in Mexico. I mean, I knew that many of the car thieves that were caught would often offer money to the officers to let them go. On the other hand, I'm sure there were also many instances where money was taken and the car thieve let go and the car taken into custody. I'm also sure there were many cases where the stolen car and the car thieve were both let go. And some of them got themselves into pretty bad situations by taking cars away from certain types of people they shouldn't have messed with. I had to take into account that I was in another country, I was a guest of theirs, and like the old saying goes "When you're in Rome you got to do as the Romans do". Be it with business people, lawyers or Law Enforcement, I never knew who I was dealing with.

But again, treating them with respect and simply being nice to everyone made a huge difference. I tried to never give my opinions about things, I never judged, placed blame or guilt or whatever the case may be.

I knew this was no joke! I remember finding out about a certain type of impound lots that were private and how they ran. Different types of impounds could be found all over Mexico. Some were private, but many were owned and run by local law enforcement agencies. These impound lots took in cars involved in crimes. They were cars taken from people that were arrested, or vehicles that were abandoned or stolen. No one was allowed into this yards. It was not unusual to see armed guards taking care of these impound yards.

My strategy was simple regardless of who the person in charge was, or who owned the yard, either private or otherwise, I would approached the low paid workers. Sometimes they were civilian individuals and at times they were security guards or law enforcement personnel from the agency that owned the yard. I knew that it made no difference if they were police or normal citizens, the fact was that they were low ranking law enforcement officers and low income employees.

I often stopped by the lots and I would take them lunch and some sodas or sometimes I'd give them 1 or 5 dollars (5-25 pesos depending on the exchange rate) so they could buy their own lunch later on. Every time I would pass by there I would try to make it a point to stop and chat with them. This was regardless if I had business there or not. After a while they would get accustomed to seeing me there. They would ask me if I was there to check on a car or if wanted to look around the impound yard. "No, no" I would say, "I just came by to say hi to you and bring you some sodas, I know it's hot and you guys work a lot." I would spend a few minutes just asking about their families or other personal things.

It's amazing to see how much trust I would gain. I gained their respect and they always wanted to help and please me. Every time I visited them they opened the door and let me in, they'd help me out, and give me whatever information I wanted. Even when they were not authorized to do so.

It's unbelievable how many times I got intelligence from these guards. The vigilance in these places was usually very tough.

They wouldn't even let you look through the fence. For the most part anyone wanting to go into one of these impounds would need to first have with them written permission from headquarters with a copy of their identification. And once they went inside they were escorted to the specific car that they wanted to look at. If they didn't have the written permission from headquarters they couldn't come in. But with me it was different. They would allow me free range of the impound yard and in some occasions they would lead me to new cars that just came in or to cars that they suspected might be stolen.

When dealing with government owned impound yards, it was amazing how in some cases the lowest guy in the scale working there would surprisingly two or three years later turn out to be the commander in charge of the whole place. You never knew when someone who was nobody one day, would be the big chief the next day. And if you treated him wrong, he'd remember that and if you treated him right, he'd remember that as well.

Such was my strategy. I always tried to keep in mind that people are people and people deserve to be treated nice, not just the high ranking officers, not just the commanders, not just the attorney generals, everybody deserves to be treated nice.

But not only did I use this system with impound yards, I also did it in government offices, with secretaries and clean up people.

And as a side effect, it paid great dividends for me throughout the seventeen years that I worked Mexico, in many, many ways.

S/A Camacho training Mexican Federal Highway Patrol

Training Mexican Army

Chapter 7
Maintaining Relationships

A BM: *So Mr. Camacho you forged these relationships that allowed you to build these networks within law enforcement in Mexico that led to a successful return of over 10,000 cars. Now can you give us a specific example of a friendship, a relationship that you forged forward that can give us an insight on what gave you the effectiveness that you had working there.

EC: I developed many relationships or friendships within the 17 years I worked in Mexico and especially since I was working in seven Mexican States. Let me tell you, it was not easy to maintain the relationships. To begin with you must take into consideration that I was working with numerous law enforcement personal from various agencies including Municipal, State and Federal and personnel would frequently change. Considering that each State would have an average of 4 main cities, it was almost impossible to maintain relationships with so many different people from so many agencies. So, I concentrated more within the State and Federal officers, although I would never shy away the municipalities.

Throughout the years I did manage established some very good contacts. And this was not just within the law enforcement community.

One day they were there, the next day they were gone and then suddenly they would reappear, possible in some other city, state or agency. Sometimes it was due to elections results and new people would be coming in. Sometimes it was a different political party and almost everyone was gone or simply the same party would win and a few people would leave and had to be replaced, or it was a matter of internal rotations. I also established good working relations with private individuals and companies I had to deal with.

I do recall some relationships that stand out for various reasons. I remember on one occasion when we were having trouble obtaining a release on a stolen car in Chihuahua City. It happened that for some unknown reason they were giving my vendor a hard time and wouldn't let us have the car. Even after I became directly involved they kept giving me the round around and finally they told me I had to go and talk to the assistant State Attorney General from Chihuahua. So I went out to the Attorney General's office and after waiting for a while I was allowed in and I met with Licenciado (attorney) Molina. I was not familiar with him, I hadn't yet met him. State elections had recently been held and the PAN political party had taken over the state government. This was the first time in over 80 years that the Pan had won the elections.

There was a new Governor and with that came a lot of other new personnel, especially in key positions. I introduced myself and he asked me a few questions as to who I was and what my functions were and so on. I knew he already knew, but he wanted to hear it from me.

I had with me a letter of introduction from the American Consulate, which I showed him. I had already planned of paying him a visit but I had been waiting for everyone to settle down in their new positions before I went knocking on their doors. He found out I was from El Paso and he actually spoke fluent English which in itself was no big surprise because many of the high government officials did speak English. Many of them having been educated in the U.S. He practiced speaking English with me instead of speaking in Spanish. He was very familiar with El Paso and even claimed to have some relatives living there. We talked and the more we talked the more we found things in common. We got along just fine and after a while we got down to business.

He asked how we could work together and help each other out. He wanted to make a good impression on the community and show them how this new administration, this new political party was going to be there and work for the people and do away with the corruption that plagued the State.

He did however make it a point to tell me that the previous political party had left the State broke. He told me all he found in his desk when he assumed the office was an old pencil in one of the drawers. He laughed saying that the previous party didn't take the paint off the walls because they didn't have time. We both laughed at that. I explained to him that I was willing to do whatever was needed to help him out, as long as it was legal and I was authorized to do it. He said he didn't expect any less.

When it came to the stolen cars I explained to him what I was doing in other Mexican states. It seemed he had already studied the U.S.-Mexico treaty. We talked about locating stolen U.S. cars and getting these same stolen cars released quicker so they could be returned to their rightful owner. We briefly talked about the treaty and my credentials and how I could help the police officers. We also spoke about fees and rewards. He was very understanding, cooperative and willing to work together looking for a solution to the high volume of stolen vehicles in his State. As I mentioned to him that stolen vehicles in Mexico was NOT good for Mexico. These stolen cars do not bring any money to the State. The local car dealers are unable to sell their Mexican product when there are many cheap stolen cars around. They also bring no tax money into the State coffers. I offered the same thing as I was doing in other States and he liked the idea. The treaty allowed for the transportation, paying of storage and preservation of seized stolen vehicles.

I offered and he agreed to a set fee with the conditions that these vehicles be kept in a safe place and not stripped of parts. Needless to say not only did I get the car in question out, (which was the main reason I was here) but our agreement and relationship lead to the release of many more stolen vehicles.

After that as it was customary for me I keep regular contact with him by making monthly visits for coffee and such. Whenever I was in Chihuahua City I'd try to stop and pay a visit. He came to El Paso a couple of times and I would chauffer him around. We would often go out for dinner. You could say that we became close friends. Whenever he came to El Paso his body guards would stay in Juarez by the international bridge and on his return he could call them and they would be waiting for him on the Mexican side where I would drop him off. In occasions the guards did cross into El Paso.

I introduced him to the local American law enforcement agencies in El Paso and we had regular meeting to see how we could all function better and help each other.

He was a real politician and a few years later he ran for Federal Senator and the guy made it. He went all the way to Mexico City. We continued keeping in touch. The good thing was that he recommended me to the person who took his place. Every two or three months he could come to Chihuahua City (he had his home and family there) and he would call me or I'd call him to see how things were going and on occasions if practical we would meet.

I remember I invited him and his staff during one of his visits to Juarez to come to El Paso for dinner. I had an expense account for entertainment (I was always over budget) and I took them to eat at Cattleman's steak house in El Paso and he loved that place. He loved that place so much he'd tell everybody that if they ever came over to El Paso to go see Camacho, "He will take you to one of the best place you can eat, the biggest, juiciest steak in Texas"

I learned later on that he would frequent Cattlemen's with his family and political friends. Our relationship continued as a matter of fact up to the day I retired. I haven't heard from him in about a year now but, he is still around, I read about him in the papers occasionally. .

Some of the high ranking officials from various States and Agencies with whom I had established a relationship would often come down to El Paso for shopping with their families. My wife and I would play host. One of them even became the Federal Attorney General years later. Another one became a Federal judge. There wasn't much I couldn't get done with such contacts in Mexico. Whenever I had a problem my solution was usually only a phone call away.

On one occasion I remember I had some problems with the federal police in Chihuahua.

It was a new Commander that had come from Baja California I believe. I didn't hesitate to give the Senator a call and tell him I was having trouble. He then asked me who I had been dealing with and I responded that I had spoken to the local Commander and the Federal Attorney. "Ok", he said. A couple of hours later that local Federal Attorney called me asking if I could go over for a meeting. He told me that he received a call from Mexico City and was told that he was supposed to help me with whatever I needed.

Behold, from then on I never had any more problems with that office. Needless to say I tried to become friends with that Attorney but it seemed he didn't hold kindly to me going over his head. This would happen sometimes.

So this is how making relationships helped me to form a strong network system to my advantage. I must admit that I always worried that I was making enemies with some who were jealous or felt I was getting too big for my britches, or just simply didn't like me ,either for being an American (some didn't care much for Mexican Americans) or because I would go over their heads.

On another occasion I was doing training for the State Police Academy in Juarez, Mexico. At that time it was one of the first established academies in the area.

There was a student named Victor who seemed very focus and interested in the topic I was teaching as he kept asking questions and interacting throughout my presentation. It was not only Auto theft that I tough, in occasions that wanted me to talk about other subjects or investigations or simply the way the U.S. Law Enforcement and the criminal system works.

Anyway talking about Victor, he continued asking questions and eventually this led to a friendly relationship that Victor and I maintain for many years. Whenever I ran into him we would go have coffee or a hard drink. We develop a pretty good relationship just by socializing, he wasn't much of a beer drinker.

For a while I lost track of him as he moved around different stations around Chihuahua. We didn't see each other as frequently as we did when he was in Juarez. About three years later he was promoted and he became the shift commander for the Juarez auto theft unit. One or two years later I remember he asked me if I was going to Torreon and I responded "yes, why?"

He said, "I hear you're going to Torreon to do some training." I said "no, not really I'm going to Gomez Palacios. How did you hear about that?" Either way he was interested, regardless if Palacios or Torreon. Actually, he asked if he could go with me. I told Victor jokingly, "why the hell do I need you for." He said, "I need to get out of here for a while man, take me with you I'll help you in whatever I can." I agreed and told him the dates we would be leaving. Victor was eager to go with me but still he needed for me to write up a request for the Attorney General saying that I needed him to go with me. As a favor I did it, which was somewhat unusual. I did it to help him due to the good friendship that we had. This was not something that I would usually do. I made a letter requesting from the Attorney General that she allow me to take Victor with me to go do some training in Torreon, as I needed his help. Torreon is in the Mexican State of Coahuila and Gomez

Palacios is in Durango which are neighboring States. Gomez Palacios and Torreon are only divided by a river. They are both over 800 kilometers from Juarez. (1 kilometer equals 0.6214 miles)

So, I had also invited a detective from the El Paso Police department named Rick. Since it was going to be a week long course I usually invited someone from the El Paso Police or Texas DPS to help me out. This time it happened to be Rick who was going to accompany me. We both went together to pick up Victor. We picked him up at the headquarters in Juarez real early in the morning and we went together in my car all the way to Torreon which was an eight (8) hour drive. I drove, as was usually the case.

We were there a week. Overall the training went well and we head it back to the U.S. On our way back he called a police unit to pick him up as we came close to the city limits of Juarez. We said bye to each other and he left with the Mexican police unit and Rick and I left to cross into the United States.

Two or three days later I called him on the Nextel cell phone and he wouldn't answer. I kept calling and calling and he wouldn't answer. A few days went by and I went to the headquarters in Juarez for something and I look for him. The radio dispatcher told me he was not there that he had been transferred. I said "what do you mean he's been transferred?" According to the dispatcher Victor had to leave right away because he was having problems. I was startled by the news. I didn't hear from him for about two weeks until one day out of the blue sky he called me on my Nextel.

He sounded happy and he told me he was now stationed in Cuauhtémoc. I said "Why Cuauhtémoc?" "Because I got transferred over here", he said. I said, "Well what the heck happen? What did you do wrong?"

He responded, "It's nothing, I'll explain later on when I see you." Later on I talked to one of his old partners and he tells me, "You know Victor is in some trouble." I said, "What do you mean?" He said Victor had been threatened by a cartel, he was told to leave the State or he was going to get killed. So he was trying to find his way out. That's when I put two and two together and figured that when he asked me to take him to Torreon he was actually hiding. I figured he used me to get him out of the State. I thought what kind of a friend is this guy. You know I never did get to talk to Victor after that. He had been living in a small farming community named Ascension close to Juarez where he had moved with his family.

He came home from Cuauhtémoc one weekend for the birthday party of his six year old son and I'm told that after the party when people had left he went outside to move his unmarked police unit back into his premises and they were already waiting for him. He was shot quite a few times with an automatic weapon while inside his car. I happened to see the car later on and it must have had thirty or forty bullet holes. They hit him on the head a couple of times and of course Victor died. Strangely enough he was wearing a cap with the letters FBI on front. I saw the cap inside the car on the floor board full of blood.

I guess those that were looking for him finally did find him. It's kind of hard to get away when they are looking for you in Mexico, those cartels eventually, they'll get to you, and they'll take care of you. In retrospect, I remembered that Victor had asked me for help trying to get visas for his family. I was going to try and help him at the American Consulate but never quite got to it and I learned later some other agency was helping him. He never did get them and I always wondered why. I recommended some contacts for visas and they would usually get them. Of course everything had to be on the up and up, usually it was a matter of moving them up the line so they wouldn't have to wait for so long. That was another thing that helped me make relationship and contacts.

In Victor's case something happened that he was unable to get them. Many contacts wanted Visas because in case of any trouble they could come to the safety of the U.S. You know many of the politicians and high ranking law enforcement officials from Mexico, actually live in El Paso and commute every day back and forth. I think Victor was planning on doing that, once he settled in the United States but unfortunately he was never able to do. Victor was a good contact and with the exception of who was after him, I always felt he would always tell me everything, or at least I thought he did.

But Victor and Molina were not the only people I became close friends with, there were others. Within the 17 years I worked in Mexico I saw many come and go for various reasons. Then there were those close friends that didn't make it like Ricalday, Licon, Saldaña, his partner Ramirez, and others.

Victor Olivas 3rd from left, Francisco Licon behind

The police car in which Cmte. Olivas was killed

Chapter 8
Networking

A BM: *Now Mr. Camacho you also had to be successful in returning in 10,000 cars you had to build rapport and work the network that you created give me another specific example of how you worked that network to successfully bring back a car to America.

E.C. Sure, first let me say that these cars, like I mentioned before, ended up in the impound yards maybe because they were stolen or were taken there because they were involved in some other criminal activity. Many times the authorities didn't even know they had a stolen vehicle in their possession at the time of impoundment.

Of course there were also times when an officer would call me just before he stopped a car for some violation or suspicion or imminently after the stop and would ask me for the status of the car in the U.S. This was very true of Officers who had been to one of my training sessions and specially those working traffic like the Federal Highway Patrol. Many times it was the training that I had given them that arouse their suspicion, and very often it was pretty good as the car would turn out to be stolen and they would take it into custody right there and then.

I recall once a Federal Highway Patrol Officer called me late one evening while I was at home.

I had already retired and was working as a private investigator. I was able to obtain registration information on Texas plates he gave me. I did not have excess to the National nor State stolen file computers as I did when I was working. But whenever a car was stolen there would usually be a stolen notation on the registration, a red flag. If I needed more information I would contact one of my contacts at TDPS (Texas Department of Public Safety) or El Paso PD or EPSO(El Paso Sheriff office) . Anyway, I received the call and the officer gave me the Texas license plate number. I told him there was no stolen notation on the 1989 Nissan. He then tells me, "No, this is not Nissan, it's an Audi and it's a practically a brand new one." He said. "Those plates you are giving me are on a Nissan. "I tell him. He then tells me he is going to stop the vehicle, apparently he was doing a rolling check.

Later he calls me and gives me the Vehicle identification Number (VIN) to the car and it was registered here in El Paso to a female. It was a two year old Audi, but there was no stolen notation. I gave him the information (not the owners name nor address) and he said, "It's got to be stolen."The guy that's driving it was an ex-federal highway patrol officer who had been fired and he had no paperwork pertaining to the vehicle. Since it's a violation in Mexico to drive with fraudulent plates he was going to store the vehicle, but was unable to take the driver into custody because there was no stolen report. I agreed and left it at that.

The following day I followed up and was able to contact the registered owner by phone and learn that in fact it had been stolen. The lady told me that about three months before she and her husband had crossed into Juarez Mexico and they were stopped by two armed individuals who made them exit the car. They stole her purse with money, credit cards, I.D. and cell phones. They also stole her husband's wallet. They asked for the keys and told them they were taking the car which they did and on the key chain were the keys to their house and business. They were told NOT to call the police nor report the car stolen, otherwise they would be back. They knew who they were, they knew where they lived and they would get them. So in fear of their lives they had not reported the car stolen. I asked them to make the report otherwise they wouldn't be able to get the car back. The lady refused since she was scared for her life and that of her husband. All this time they were still making car payments and paying insurance. Anyway, to make a long story short I helped them out and got the car back, but it took me almost three more months.

As I mentioned before some of the law enforcement agencies would have their own impound lot. May it be city or state owned and for the most part they would charge either very little for storage and towing fees, or none at all.

But there were those that didn't have a yard and would contract with private storage facilities, since they didn't have their own. The "Federal Highway patrol and other federal agencies were some of the ones that would usually contract with private yards. Now those were a problem because they were not controlled by the municipality or law enforcement agency that utilized them to store cars.

My network of contacts and networking were not only with law enforcement, but with private Individuals and companies as well.

In one occasion for example I was told by an officer about this car in Tepic. It seemed that this officer had stored a Jeep Cherokee after he found out it had been stolen. It had been taken to the storage facility for safe keeping. Since I was in the area of Tepic I went over to the private facility to take a look at the Jeep. It was in good condition for a fresh kill, which is what we called the recently stored vehicles. They had just brought it in and close by to where it was parked, at the same location, I saw two other relatively nice looking Jeep Cherokees that were somewhat minor stripped. It is not unusual for cars to be stripped days after they are brought into some of these storage facilities, regardless if private or government owned. And like always, nobody knows anything of what happened or who did it.

Anyway, I asked the owner of the facility about the other two jeeps pointing to them (he was walking with me in the yard) and he said "oh well I don't know they've been here for a while."

I asked if I could check them out and he agreed. So I checked them and sure enough they were also stolen. They were 4 or 5 years old at the time and had been stolen for about the same amount of time.

I now had three stolen Jeep Cherokees, a fresh one in real good condition and two partially stripped ones, but still worth something to someone. Since they had been stolen for a while, they now belonged to some insurance companies I was sure. I looked up the information and it fact they were now registered to some insurance companies. I contacted the insurance companies and I sent them some photos and told them of the conditions and storage fees. They did not want the stripped ones back. They told me to do as I pleased with them because the cost of bringing them back would not be beneficial. They would simply write them off and close the file if not already done so.

I then asked the owner of the lot how much was due for storage fees on the new jeep that was just brought in. And I don't remember how much he quoted but it was a ridiculous high amount.

I asked why such high amount and he claimed he had to tow it from a long distance away. I then asked about the two stripped ones and what the chances of getting a discount. All I got was a dance and a song. The fee was also very high because, supposedly it had involved a lot of work. I told him that I would probably just leave them there, they were too costly.

Unless, I said, he was willing to negotiate. We went back and forth and finally my last deal in this negotiation was to offer Mr. Neto (The owner of the towing company) to let me have the new jeep for free and I would give him the other two Jeeps. He asked me if I was able to do that and I confirmed that I was able to do so.

"I'll give them to you and I'll even give you an authorization letter right now saying that I donate them to you, and that they are no longer stolen" I said. My plan (which I would do sometimes when needed) was to cancel the stolen record in U.S so he won't have any problems. This could be done by contacting the Police Department that had the theft and advising them of the recovery and abandonment from the owner and I would also send pictures.

I would also ask the insurance companies, since they didn't

want the vehicle back, for the title and sometimes they would give it to me, sometimes they could not. But they would give me a letter authorizing me to dispose of the vehicle.

Mr. Neto then asked again if I could really do that and I confirmed that it was possible. He agreed to my offer and we closed the deal. I got the new stolen Jeep free of charge! After that deal with Mr. Neto, I had him calling me on a regular basis every time he would receive new cars to check to see if they were stolen. He would call me or fax me the VIN. I guess he wanted to see if he could get any more cars for free. The two stripped Jeeps were going to be abandoned anyway, but he didn't know that.

At an average I would normally return about fifty stolen vehicles per month back to the U.S. and leave behind about twenty five. This went on the 17 years period I worked Mexico.

S/A Camacho preparing to inspect vehicles
at Mexican Police impound yard.

My distinguished guest I.D. from the State Attorney

Chapter 9

Death of a Commandante

ABM: *Now Mr. Camacho you also had another friend that was a victim of the crime in Mexico, tell us a little about that.

EC: Well, I'm not sure of which one you might be referring too, I did have a large amount of friends that were victims of crimes in Mexico. Many of them I simply refer to as acquaintances or coworkers as we never got real close. Such is the case with this person that I recall now, although I knew him pretty well, I wouldn't really call him a friend. Although I had known him for years and we got along real well, I was never able to get to close to him, he kept his distance and so did I.

He was one of the supervisors who was actually Victor's boss, the guy that got shot outside his house on the day of his boy's birthday party. Victor's boss was named Dominguez and like I said before, I'd known him for years. Since I'd known him he had always been a supervisor. He had always been a *co-mandante*, (commander) he was *a* low level comandante when I first met him. It was no great secret that he was involved in crime and the rumor was that he had a place, a shop where they dismantle stolen cars and then sold the parts, A CHOP-SHOP. I figured it was counterproductive for me to try to do anything about it, after all I was not there to investigate. At least not on my own. So, I just let it go, everyone else did.

As time went on he ended up making rank and became what we called a *primer comandante (first commander)*. He wasn't liked much by other commanders, but he had someone at the very top who protected him. As a matter of fact one time when I arrived at the headquarters in Chihuahua City from El Paso, I became aware of a situation which had just occurred. As Oscar and I arrived at the *comandancia* (headquarters) as it was part of my routine whenever arriving at any Mexican City, as it was polite and customary to let them know I was in town.

Anyway, we noticed that obviously something had happened. As we approached the 1st commander's office we saw a bunch of high ranking agents and several advisors and staff personnel standing around close to the commandants office. Some people inside, some outside of the office and by the look in their faces it was obvious something had gone down. It was here that we learned that another comandante had accused Dominguez of some type of criminal activity and had called him a thief and criminal. Dominquez did not take it lightly and they both started yelling at each other and after the yelling punches were thrown and they had to be physically separated from each other before weapons were drawn.

Despite of rumors and certain accusations nothing was ever done. His only consequence after the fight was simply to be transferred to the city of Parral. I saw him in Parral later on once or twice during my travels. We never talked about that flight.

Then one day surprisingly enough, all of a sudden he ended up in Juarez as the number one commander for the whole zone. It was at this time that he was Victor's boss. I recall when Victor got killed I went to Dominguez's office to convey my condolences for Victor's death. He surprised me with this reply, "Well Camacho, you know some of these young kids just don't want to listen, they'll never learn, they don't do what they are supposed to do, so these are the consequences, what can you expect?"

That's not a reply that I expected to hear from him. Not under the situation. What he was trying to convey to me was that Victor was not complying with someone's orders, or wishes or certain other things, let's say, *he wasn't playing ball.* It was common knowledge at the time that certain officers from certain agencies were expected at times to comply with and do what was needed to protect certain cartels in Juarez. Within certain networking circles everybody knew that the State police were backing or protecting a certain cartel that was from Chihuahua. They were considered the "*homeboys.*" It was obvious they were being protective of that cartel. When it came to them helping us from the U.S it was all within limits.

Whenever there were elections a lot of factors would go into play and depending on which political party won, it could mean which cartel would rule. And it wasn't uncommon for certain loyalties to change, or there would be consequences. This sometimes entailed some cleaning and at the max, a lot of death. Or when a new cartel moved in trying to take over the area that too would cause actions on both parts, the already established group and the incoming group. Sometimes the L.E. agencies would back one or the other, or simply let them figure it out. Needless to say death was usually the result.

I guess Victor got out of hand a little bit, I don't know.

He had made some arrests and he had taken some stolen cars away from some certain people that maybe, he should not have done. And maybe that put him on the blacklist, I don't know, I'm just guessing.

Dominquez was actually from Chihuahua and he lived in Chihuahua City and that's where his family lived. About eight or nine months later I learned that he too had been killed. What apparently had happened as I was told, was that he had been in his private car off duty with his wife and his teenage daughter on this particular day. They were driving on the express way in Chihuahua when he apparently noticed that he was being followed. There were actually a couple of cars following them. He then decided to get off the express way close to one of the new shopping centers that had a Wal-Mart and a Sam's to see if they were indeed being following, or maybe to shake them off. He then turned into a side street and pulled over and stopped his car.

The other two cars stopped behind him. One stopped almost in front in a parallel position. I was told that Dominquez actually got out of his car to confront them and cussed them out. He asked them what the hell they wanted, using not so friendly words of course. I'm told there were four to six men in the cars. Dominquez told them he was with his family and asked them to respect that. At that moment one of the men that had been following him jumped in Dominquez car through the opened driver's side door. (Dominquez had left the door open and the engine running) His wife and daughter were inside the car and they were getting hysterical screaming and such. The man who had gotten into Dominquez car drove the car around the corner with his wife and daughter in the car as they screamed and begged for Dominquez life. I guess at this point both Dominquez and his family knew what was going to happen.

According to the wife and the daughter all they heard afterwards was numerous shots. Dominguez's body was left there on the middle of the street with numerous bullet wounds. According to the investigators Dominquez had been made to kneel down and was executed right there in the middle of the street. I don't know how many bullets it took to end the life of *Comandante* Dominguez. Even though Dominquez was armed, he never drew his weapon.

The irony of this is that at one point when I went over and told him about Victor he didn't show any compassion or sympathy and here he was nine months later. Who knew it was his turn. It seemed to me that after Dominquez execution there were a few more, one after the other. Why they were being executed? I really didn't know and in many of these cases I found myself puzzled. Because with some, I couldn't figure it out. Although in some of these cases I admit I almost expected it, and it was a matter of time.

Drug war results, bodies on side of roads.

Chapter 10
Mexican Police Structure

A BM:*Comandante is the equivalent of what here?

EC: A Commandante is no more than a Commander. Just like in the U.S. many of the Police Agencies call their supervisors Commanders. Although they are all Commanders, there are different levels. For example you can call a sergeant, a commanders, or a lieutenant can also be a commander. But there are agencies that actually have a rank of Commander.

With very few exceptions, the Mexican States, divide their states into Police sections. Using Chihuahua as an example, the state of Chihuahua is divided into four (4) sections, they are the Central, North, South, and the West. Usually the main headquarters will be within the City Capital of the State and each section will have a regional command police station, who in turn can have various smaller police sub stations within its section or region.

The person who runs the whole State Police is usually referred to as the Director who can have one or two sub-directors. In Chihuahua the commander in charge of a region is called a 1st Commandante. (Primer) Who will have a 2nd Commandte (*Segundo comandante*) as second in command.

The men sometimes (in larger cities) are broken into

groups, sometimes to deal with a specific crime such as Auto Theft. In this case, each group will have its own Commandante who is known as El Commandante de Grupo. You could always equate a Commandante de grupo, to a sergeant.

Smaller stations in remote areas are often run by a Commandante de Grupo and all investigations are done by the same men. Or if it's large enough it will have a 2nd Cmte. They don't have the luxury of being broken down into specific type of investigators.

The Federal Police, being national will break down into States. A State will have one Commander, (usually in the State Capital) then smaller stations in larger cities.

For the most part, anyone with supervisory authority is sometimes referred to as a Commandante.

Important to say is that the Mexican State Police work under the State Attorney General. The Federal Police work under the Federal Attorney general.

So whenever you have a main station, be it in the Capital or within the region headquarters, you will have a State Deputy Attorney General and a prosecutor working in that area. Same goes for the Feds.

Chapter 11
A Deadly Day

ABM: *This brings us to the end of this side of the tape and now it's time to flip the tape over to start a new fresh side of the other side.

ABM:*So Mr. Camacho you were in Mexico and you have established a good rapport, you've leverage this network of law enforcement to effectively return well over ten thousand cars back to the United States. And now you want to take it a step further to aid your comrades in Mexico to kind of coordinate a more centralized approach to crime prevention specifically car theft on the Mexican border. This led to a very historic day in your life what we call, really the deadliest day that you've experienced as a peace officer. Take it from there please.

EC:Yeah, I have been telling you of how I had many friends, many commanders and officers that I became very close with. Well, I guess no one was closer than Ricalday. Ricalday was kind of special to me, let me give a little background here.

As years went by and I was trusted more and more by Mexican law enforcement, I started to bring together different law enforcement agencies, both from Mexico and the U.S.

Locally (in Juarez and in El Paso) what I had done was organize a committee of representatives of mid- management supervisors of various law enforcement agencies from both countries. I had just about every law enforcement agency in El Paso and every law enforcement agency from Juarez Mexico.

I had Federal, State, and Municipal as well as Mexican Customs. Within the Mexican Feds I had the Highway Patrol, Federal Judicial, Aduana and Federal Attorney General's office. Within the Mexican State, I had the State Judicial and State Attorney General. The Municipal I had traffic and Patrol as well as impound yards.

From the U.S. Federal Branches I had U.S. Customs and for a while the Border Patrol. From the State I had Texas, and New Mexico State Police. Within the Municipal, besides the El Paso Police Department I had other surrounding cities and colleges Police Departments. The FBI was hard to get to attend our meeting, but they knew about us as well as the DEA and Marshalls Office.

We were meeting once a month. The purpose was to get to know each other, our authority, limitations, and so forth. Establish a line of communications and exchange information so we could address problems if/when they should arise.

This way we could know who to call at any time, should something come up and we could better serve our communities respectively.

It was working tremendously well. We got to know each other, we had each other's phone and cell numbers and we could quickly communicate with each other and we better understood each other and started to develop trust as before there was a lot of suspicion and mistrust.

What led me to do this besides always thinking that we should always know who we are dealing with, was an occasion that came up when I had a call from a Texas Ranger from the Sierra Blanca area in Texas. The local police had in their custody a Mexican National for a minor offense. While in jail he was claiming to have killed a women in Juarez. He had since become a Christian and had repented for what he had done. He was willing to give a confession but didn't want to give it to just anyone from Mexico. He claimed that the Mexican police would for sure try and hang all the murders of women in Juarez on him. He wanted someone he could trust.

There was no crime committed in the U.S. so they were getting ready to turn the guy over to the Border Patrol. The U.S. officials knew they had to do something, but they had no idea who they could call in Mexico. Not until they contacted the Texas Ranger who personally knew me and who decided to give me a call since he remembered that I worked in Mexico.

After being told of what had taken place and what they wanted, I contacted one of my trusted friends who was a prosecutor with the State Attorney General office in Juarez and I explained the situation. He agreed to help. I set it up so that he could go to Sierra Blanca and interview the man before they released him.

This situation got me thinking that there are many instances where we could surely help each other out across the border and it was just a matter of knowing who to call. We couldn't be 100% self-sufficient, we needed each other. Why not get to know each other? I was fortunate enough that I knew people from both sides. So, I began by inviting everyone I could think of with the help of the American Consulate in Juarez and we got our little committee going. I used the American Consulate because in case someone didn't know me personally, the American Consulate being a Representative of the United States Government was respected and trusted in Mexico.

But after a while, and seeing how good it was working, I wanted to take it a step further. What I did was set up a meeting in Chihuahua City, which is the capital of the state of Chihuahua By the way, in the event you don't know Chihuahua is the largest State in Mexico, it's their Texas.

Anyway I asked the American Consulate in Juarez to help me make an official invitation to the neighboring Mexican States. I must say that I got tremendous help from the people at the American Consulate every time I needed their help. I must also say that the other two American Consulate offices I worked with, Monterrey and Guadalajara were also very helpful when I needed them.

As I told you before I worked in other Mexican states besides the state of Chihuahua, so I wanted to get them involved as well. I pretty much knew who to contact in each State, so it was kind of easy to make this work.

I had a real good response to the invitations from different Mexican Law Enforcement Agencies that I decided to also invite people from the Mexican insurance industry. I also invited just about any other business or industry that dealt with the Auto Industry. Following the already established formation of the International Association of Auto Theft Investigators in the United States , which is composed of not only Law Enforcement but just about anyone who deals with the automobile industry, I included the Mexican dealerships. I thought it was time to bring together both police and community, especially business people who are greatly affected. Not only because of the loss of money, but on some cases their health as well. I knew everyone played an important role in this cause.

We met in a Hotel in Chihuahua, they loaned us a large meeting room. I had such a good response that the news media got ahold of it and made a big deal. They were all over the place and although we were able to keep them out while we had our meeting, no sooner had we broken off that they poured in. I tried staying away from interviews, preferring that the Mexican authorities speak to the press, but later on I saw my name in the newspaper. They were saying that I was going to help the police to do away with drug cartels and crime and a bunch of boloney I never said! The news media!

Anyway, at this meeting which was attended by people as far away as Mexico City were my old friends from the State of Durango, Ricalday, and his cousin the State Attorney General.

I had met Ricalday years before. He was now the State Police Director for the State of Durango. When I first met him he was just like, I guess you can say a rooky in a training. He was attending one of my training sessions in Gomez Palacios. That had been ten years before. Now he was the number one man. I must admit I was very proud of him, especially since he was so correct and faithful to his job. He was a nonsense individual and did not like corruption.

I remember him when I first met him, as this tall skinny guy coming up to me and asking me some questions. It seemed that in every break we had he would come over and talk to me some more. He was very curious about many of the things I was talking about. Within time we became close, and our relationship went beyond work. We knew each other's family, he loved his family and often spoke of the future. He visited El

Paso and me often.

Throughout the years we kept contact. I saw him going up the ranks. One day his cousin became the attorney general for the State of Durango. Well, guess who becomes the regional commander, for the whole State of Durango? Ricalday was the right choice. And guess who ended up being his advisor? Me, of course! I ended up being his advisor because of the trust and the friendship that we had established throughout the years. He became very, very instrumental in helping me explain and support ideas I had to help us all be more effective in our work. During our meetings we would brain storm and problem solve issues.

After our meeting in Chihuahua City with all the different agencies and others and the proposals I made, the attorney general, his cousin, loved the idea of what we were doing. He even offered to propose our ideas at their next Attorney General's meetings. All the state Attorney Generals from throughout the Republic of Mexico met regularly and he was going to bring up my suggestion.

He felt confident that if we presented this at their next meeting, they would be more than willing to help us create an organization at the national level. He believed that this would be a good way to get us together and be able to communicate and have an exchange of information between States.

This was not only going to help the State , because unfortunately at the time, a lot of municipalities didn't have contact or anything to do with the State police, and the state had nothing to do with other States or the Federal police. Traditionally these agencies always kept to themselves and this was a way we could all get together in the same band wagon. And in the process the municipal police would be included and could benefit from this, although there was some hesitation as they were not very well trusted.

Corruption ran very high within the municipal police, who by the way was a preventative police and not an investigative organization. They were also the lowest paid.

I had always noticed throughout the years that there were a lot of good police officers that I had met who really wanted to do the right thing and fight crime and such, you know. They believed in what they were doing, so I figured this is the time, this is the time to get them together and maybe together we could do some good. We agreed and decided we would have another pre-meeting in Durango before approaching the association of Mexican State Attorney General's in their upcoming meeting.

The pre-meeting was going to be only between the attorney general in Durango, his staff, Ricalday and me, so that we could set some ground work as to how to approach the Attorney Generals and outline our presentation. As the time was approaching I worked my schedule out so I could take care of some business in Torreon then I figured since the city of Durango is only 255 kilometers away I would stay overnight in Torreon then continue to Durango.

In Torreon I had a meeting with one of my assistants and stayed in Gomez Palacios that night. The next day I had a breakfast meeting in Torreon with some people which took longer than I expected.

After wards I met again with my assistant and didn't get to head out of Gomez Palacios till around 2pm. In Durango I always stayed at the Holiday Inn Express because it was right on the main road coming into Durango, just before you go into all the high traffic area. As I was getting close Durango around 4 or 5 pm I call Ricalday on the Nextel.

I told him "Hey *comandante* I'm coming into town." The Nextel is actually a cell phone but it also works as walkie-talkie, it's a phone we use within the Mexican communication system and all law enforcement officers for the most part had one.

It was a way of communicating for those who were not on the police band or to avoid it.

He asked me where I was going to stay and what time I would arrive to the hotel. I responded that I was staying at the same place I always stay at and that I would be there in less than an hour. He then told me to go ahead and check in when I get there and to let him know my room number. He then told me he would call me back because he was tied up with some things. He wanted to come by and pick me up to possibly go have dinner with the attorney general and get things rolling.

I felt great! I knew this was going to be a good opportunity to create something new and great.

Upon arrival to the hotel I checked in and then I called a couple of my vendors in Durango and asked them to come over to the hotel so we could meet. I knew it would take them half an hour to an hour to arrive at the hotel. While waiting I decided to go across the street where they had just opened up a Wal-Mart. It is always customary to have a bottle of booze to welcome invitees. The idea was to socialize for a little bit before talking business.

Later on one of my assistants came to the hotel to brief me on what had been going on. I gave them instructions and they took off to work on some stuff. I then turned on the TV and my lap top to get some work done while I waited for Ricalday to show up.

It must have been about an hour around 6 or 7 pm when I heard this real loud knocking on the door. I open it and it was my two assistants who seemed out of breath and they ask me, "Did you hear what happened?" I replied that I had no idea what they were referring to. One of them says, "They just ambushed and killed *Comandante* Ricalday". The news shock the hell out of me. I didn't know what to say. For a few seconds I thought they were joking, but the seriousness in their faces told me it was for real. I couldn't believe it, I felt a cold sweat running up towards my face and a knot in my stomach. They asked me if I had not heard the sirens and the helicopter.

I said "No, no I didn't hear anything I've been inside my room." (The TV was kind of loud) One of them repeats almost in tears, "They killed him." Okay I said, come in sit down tell me what happened? They said they were on their way to my hotel room when they saw the commotion. They said it happened on the back of the hotel. As Ricalday was coming around the back, apparently towards my room, they were waiting for him. The ambushed him and killed him, along with the driver and his bodyguard, all three who were in the truck they say. The police truck was all shot up.

I was confused and asked them, "What we should do" and at the same time told them, "Should we go and see what we can do?" "No, no they said don't even go outside right now, it's a mess, there are police cars all over the place, they are stopping and detaining people, it's just a big mess" they said. There were cops all over the place and it was very chaotic.

They believed we shouldn't interfere and we should just let them do their job. There was nothing we could do for now and I agreed, because I trusted their opinion. They were both from Durango and although they were civilians, they were my vendors, my advisors. Not only did they help me to repatriate the stolen cars from Durango, they knew the ins and outs.

I then thought that I needed to call into U.S. I called DPS El Paso and got ahold of Lt. Mario Flores. I checked in with him and I told him what had just happened. Mario also knew Ricalday from previous meetings. Since my commission came from The Department of Public Safety, as a special Texas Ranger, I thought I should inform him as he was my immediate supervisor. Lt. Flores said, "You get your ass back here immediately!" I asked him about staying for the funeral services. We had a discussion over the phone for a while and eventually being that we did not know what was really going on, we didn't know what led to this situation or if I was meant to be there, Lt. Flores told me to come back to El Paso immediately or as soon as I could.

I told him it was kind of late to leave that night, but I would be leaving first thing in the morning. I gave some money to my assistant, I told him that I had to leave first thing in the morning that I was sure there was going to be a rosary and funeral, to buy some flowers on my behalf and take it to them. I asked them to please keep me inform.

That night I could hardly sleep and it must have been 4:30 or 5 in the morning when I finally got up, checked out and drove the 645 miles back to El Paso only stopping to get gas. I kept thinking, why. Why? And what if it had happened after Ricalday had picked me up.

Mexican and U.S. Police meeting Cmte.
Ricalday 3ʳᵈ from right

Police truck where Cmte. Ricalday was killed

Chapter 12

Reasoning the death of Ricalday

A BM:*Do you have any opinions of why he was killed? Who killed him and why?

EC: I don't really know. It's hard to say, and I would hate to speculate. But if I had to guess, well, I would have to say, I do have a couple of opinions.

You see, a few months prior to him being killed, Ricalday had seized a huge shipment. I'm talking about one of those huge 5 ton trucks that was fully loaded with marijuana that apparently had just come down form the mountains. As the Director /Regional Commander, he was one of the main ones that made the call to go ahead with the seizing of the cargo. In Mexico, for the most part unless the commander orders the troops they will not act. A check with their commander is always in order. Why, you may ask? The reason is self-explanatory.

I mean it's rare for lower level officers to take action on their own. It could very well be that it's a protected cargo. Ricalday played an instrumental role on the marijuana being seized. After the truck and drugs had been taken into custody

I was told by a mutual friend who also worked with him, that he had been threatened, he had been told that he better release that load or else. He was the type that would say, hell no I'm not doing that. He was not afraid and he couldn't be intimidated. I also heard from a close friend of his that he had told his cousin that for the last few days he thought he was being followed. His cousin told him to get more body guards, but he refused. As far as I knew him he was straight and was trying to do a good job for the State of Durango. Maybe that was the reason, maybe it was one of the drug cartels, and after all, that was a huge loss for them. They might have tried to buy him off and they were unable too. I mean if you lose a truck load of a four or five tons that's a lot- a lot of dope. And buying off is usually the first option, then its threats, then of course what follows. They don't make hollow threats.

Another case that also happened some months prior, in which I was also involved, was the seizure of a stolen Hummer. I was informed of a satellite hit on a stolen Hummer. Satellite hits are run by a couple of companies in the United States that for a fee will install an GPS application on your vehicle so if it is stolen they can activate it and the satellite can trace the stolen car's movements anywhere it goes. In some cases they can even kill the engine. When a stolen car sends a signal to the company they inform the local law enforcement agency, but in this case, since it was in Mexico and it was in my area of responsibility, I got the call. We had previously recovered a couple of stolen vehicles in Juarez by these means and Victor had helped us with them. They were also located by the signal given by the apparatus. On this particular case I had gotten a call about a Hummer that was stolen in California and the drop was coming from Juarez.

I remember calling Victor and giving him the coordinates, latitude and longitude of the location of the vehicle. I remember him going over there and he couldn't find it. I thought that maybe it was because he gone to the place 24 hours after I had given him the location and it had been moved. His men checked all around the area from where the drop was coming from. I recall Victor telling me he couldn't find it and after a while the signal seemed to go and had gone dead. The only thing we could think of at the time was that maybe it was inside an enclosure or maybe they had found the gadget that sends the signal or something like that.

Couple of days later I get another call about the same vehicle, but this time the drop was close to City of Parral Chihuahua and it appeared to be on the move moving in a southern direction. Now Parral is real close to Durango. It's almost on the border with Durango on the western edge by the mountains. There is a 2 lane road that most consider the back door because it's an alternative to the main highway which starts in Juarez which is Highway 45 which goes through Camargo, Delicias all the way to Durango. It is a very heavily traveled local highway.

I can describe the highway as a road with two lanes and it goes through small towns, zig -zagging around the mountains. It has a lot of curves and it's hilly.

I was periodically kept informed as to the location of the vehicle as it was being driven. I was informed that they were still keeping track of the vehicle and it was still continuing south. All I could hope for was that it was not being taken all the way to Mexico City. I really needed to get it stopped before it got any further away. But I didn't know where it was destined and stopping it on the highway was difficult. I was told they would keep track on it and alert me if it's stopped, which was our best option.

Nothing happened the rest of that day until I received a call the following day and I was informed that this time the vehicle had made a stop in a small city named Maria Del Oro in the State of Durango. Maria Del Oro is west from the city of Durango. This time the vehicle was stationary. Since it was in Durango, I called Ricalday to update him. Ricalday immediately made contact with his people at Maria Del Oro with instructions to look for the Hummer. So about one hour or so later he called me back to say that some of his people were reporting the Hummer as being in a car wash and apparently there are a couple of individuals cleaning it out. Ricalday was on the radio with some of his agents in Maria Del Oro and I could hear the conversation. I could hear the agents asking for the VIN (vehicle identification number) and color.

Do you have the VIN number? Ricalday asked. Yes I said and I provided the information so he could pass on to his people. Ricalday informed me that they would check it out and call me later. About half an hour later or so he calls me back to say that that was not the Hummer that I was looking for. I said, "That's got to be it, we are not going to get a drop on a vehicle that's not the vehicle." Ricalday said the VIN number was different and did not match. The Hummer they were inspecting had a different VIN. I then realized that they had probably switched the numbers. So I told him, "you know what, they switched it, they had time, maybe that's what they were doing in Juarez when we lost the drop." It all made sense, they brought it in to

Juarez and they took it in somewhere and they worked on it to change the numbers. I then asked, "what about the confidential number, I thought that some of your people knew how to do that?" He said he was not quite sure where to find it and he did not think the guys knew either. I gave Ricalday instructions on how to locate the number and waited for him to get back to me. The Hummer was the same color, it had to be it.

The location of confidential numbers was something I usually didn't teach or talk about, it was something I would mention on a need to know bases.

It was getting kind of late and Ricalday had not called me back so I left my office for the day thinking he would probably call me later on my cell should anything come up. But he didn't call me till early the next day to confirm that indeed it was the stolen Hummer.

However, Ricalday was resistant to take action on retrieving it, he said that some heavy dudes had it and his men didn't know what to do or if they should do anything at all. Ricalday knew of its location and they had identified who had it, but had not taken any action, I told him, "You know what *comandante* if it's going to be a problem for you or for your men, back off. A Hummer is not worth the lives of your men" "Camacho", he said, "these dudes are heavy, I mean, the men, they are powerful. I might have to do some negotiation with them." Once he said "heavy dudes" I knew that he was referring to, someone very influential, somebody either real rich, a politician or someone who is part of a cartel. You know, the ones with the money. By past experiences those were the ones that were using the Hummers. Ricalday then said, "Well, let me see what I can I do, I'll call you back." I reminded him that if he needed to back off to go ahead and do it.

So the next day early in the morning by 9 o'clock he calls me to inform me that the Hummer was on his way down, they had retrieved it.

I asked if it had caused any problems for them and he said "not a big deal, we'll straighten this out, don't worry about it." Ricalday said it would be deliver in Durango in a couple hours.

I later found out that he had to negotiate with them a deal on the tires and mirrors that they had claim to have put on the Hummer. Ricalday knew what he was doing, there wasn't a thing I could have said. But a stolen vehicle to a cartel is no big thing, usually they would give them up without much trouble, they had plenty of them.

Now if he was murdered because of that or because of that huge load that he had seized, I don't know. Or if it was because of the meeting we were going to have, again I don't know. I think in either case, to take out a State Police Director, it's got to be someone big, the order came from some heavy dude.

And to take him out the way they did, with the force that they did, it was almost unbelievable, they wanted to make sure he was dead and that a message was send.

From what I was told, behind the hotel there's a high speed bump. (I hardly ever drove through the back) The attackers were waiting right by the speed bump, they knew that to pass by this area it meant the person would have to slow down when they approached. The attackers were in two vehicles waiting by the speed bumps, one on each side with automatic weapons. Both vehicles opened fire at the same time. They "Swiss cheesed" the truck along with the occupants. They apparently knew his movements. They knew exactly where he was going and the route. They knew where he was going, and I wonder, did they know who he was meeting with? If so, how?

I always felt there was some inside leak. You know, whoever did it, it's not going to be an individual that has a personal grudge against him, nothing like that, I don't think. It had to be somebody big, some type of organized group and they wanted to make sure they send a message out. But again, it could have been something else that I was not aware of, or it could have been that he was cooperating too much with me (the U.S.), maybe it was about the gathering of different law enforcement agencies that we were trying to get started. I just don't know. I have asked myself over and over, why? I've been asked since then if I felt that I too was a target as well, no, I don't think so.

Executed Mexican State Police with a narco message

Chapter 13
Returning to the U.S.

ABM *So that night that Ricalday was killed right in the back of the hotel that you were staying at and he was coming to meet with you and you found out that they were police helicopters a heavy police presence there in the hotel how did you deal with the rest of the evening and even in your drive away from the hotel that next morning?

EC: I must confess I didn't sleep much that night. Of all the friends I had lost to that point, Ricalday was the one who affected me more. I wondered a lot about a lot of things. I wondered about the motives behind this attack. Why Ricalday, I mean, I just didn't see it coming, it made no sense. I didn't see anything that could have warned me that something was wrong. The way he acted, Ricalday did not believe or think that anything was going to happen to him(I guess none of us do) And I must admit that it crossed my mind a couple of times, that maybe it was because of me . I don't know.

I contemplated on staying a day or two because I knew that there would be funeral arrangements and church services in the next few days. In Mexico dead people are interned quickly.

It is very customary in Mexico to bury an individual within a day or two. It's real quick. I really wanted to call the

Lieutenant and the organization I worked for to ask them to allow me stay so that I could go to the rosary and the funeral. I mean I felt like that was the least I could do, go to the funeral services, and make a presence. Ricalday was a good friend. How could a friend of mine be killed like that and I just disappear? I felt like I was a coward, I was going to be running away , however, by the same token part of me kept saying you know, there is nothing you really can do. Is anyone going to blame you? Maybe it would be wise to leave and check with the vendors later to see how things are. I figured I could always come back to visit his family including his cousins to give them my condolences.

But right now, I was in a position that I didn't want to be in. Didn't quite know what to go about it, but I knew that coming back to El Paso was the right thing to do, and my orders.

On my drive back to El Paso I kept thinking about it. One thing that kept coming back to me was the newspaper article in Chihuahua that had been written about me a month or so before when we had that big meeting. I never read the article but some friends from Chihuahua had and they felt that it made me look like a threat, the things the reporters wrote seemed as if I was going to use the Mexican Law Enforcement Officers to rid Mexico of Crime and Cartels. That I was leading the charge. That made me wonder!

Mexican Federal Police station attacked by cartel
Notice bullet holes on building

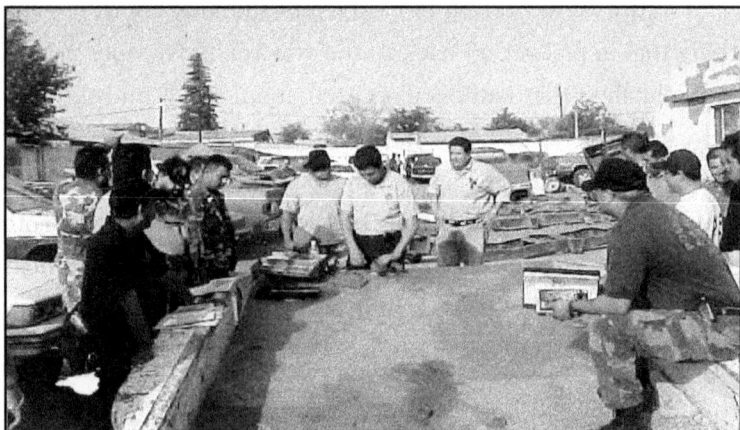

S/A Camacho conducts hands on training in
Casas Grandes Mexico for State Police Investigators.

Chapter 14
What is the border problem?

ABM *Now Mr. Camacho you have experienced quite a
bit in your journey as a police officer as a Navy petty officer as an investigator and as an agent. Tell us a little bit about
how bad the problem of car theft is on the border, how big of
a problem is it, what is the future of law enforcement combating this major issue, and how can the average person protect
themselves?

EC: First, as far as the problem along the border, it's really
no difference along the border then it is in Seattle, Chicago, or
anywhere else when it comes to Auto Theft. We all may have
a problem, but simply due to the fact that we are so close to
Mexico that is what makes a difference. With the exception of
the numbers, I mean when it comes to stolen vehicles, and the
recovery rate, I think that is what makes a difference.

If you are talking of other types of crime, I don't think living next to Mexico is really is a problem. Many who are not
familiar with the area may think that violence and other crimes
spill into the U.S. Cities along the border, but I don't think so.
That of course with the exception of the movement of drugs.

But speaking of car theft lets take for example, in Chicago
or anywhere in the United States there is a cushion (so to

speak) to help you as a police officer to recover that vehicle. What I mean is that all surrounding cities and law enforcement officers can easily become aware of that stolen car in minutes. That car will remain in U.S. soil for hours or days. The technology used by U.S. law enforcement can usually detect the car before it goes too far unless it's stationary and enclosed. That in its self helps in the location and recovery of the stolen vehicle.

Sadly, here in the border (El Paso) as it is with just about every border city, with a close proximity with Mexico, it only takes a matter of 15 or 20 minutes to get from any point within the city and across into Mexico. And once in Mexico thieves are clear and free to do as they like. U.S. police cannot touch them and as a matter of fact, all they can do is rely on the Mexican authorities to do their job. And for this you need cooperation, you need contacts and a good working relationship. This in its self will not guarantee you anything, but it does help. Especially true if corruption in the area is high within the Mexican Law Enforcement agencies.

Many of these cars going into Mexico don't stay in the border, they are transported further in. In some occasions they are shipped out of the country from Mexico sea ports.

Now, what has been the norm along the border cities for years and years is the easy pickings that the thief has. Now, I'm not saying that all thieves are Mexican Nationals, no, we have our own, but we have found that this scenario happens very often regardless if it's someone coming from Mexico or its one of our own home grown thieves. Also many of these thieves are drug users who trade the stolen vehicle for drugs, or they are drug pushers who do the same.

The thieve will travel through and check our the shopping centers, or other places where people frequently park their cars during daylight hours and looks for either an easy pick, or a specific type of vehicle that may be on his list. In some cases he can even pick the color.

At night it is also common that a thief will wonder into the neighborhoods of the city to steal a car. Nighttime social gathering places are also a good place to look for vehicles. You know that the owner is going to be there for a while. For the most part these individuals already know what type of car or truck they are looking for, it's not unusual for them to have a shopping list. The thieves usually come in groups of 3-4 and have a driver who drops them off.

Although this method still occurs in many occasions, it has been changing.

It has not change completely but what the thieves are doing now is waiting in the Mexican side for the American citizens to go shopping or dining and steal the car or truck from them while in Mexico.

This is what is known Carjacking a very dangerous event. This way, among other reasons, they stand less of a chance of being caught and being prosecuted. And because most carjackers are carrying weapons, I foresee this auto theft situation becoming more violent. Why is the trend moving in that direction? You may ask. It's a combination of things. As U.S. Law Enforcement makes it tougher for the thieve and as manufacturers make it more difficult to steal a car and as car owners are utilizing more methods of securing their vehicles with cut-off switches, alarms, transponder keys, etc., the car thieve has no choice. It surely makes it more difficult to steal a car.

So now the car owner must be more alert, and be on the lookout for carjackers. If they cannot break into it and get it running, they have to look for other means. They will wait at a stop light, at a corner, or a parking lot and then approach the car owner with a weapon and take the car by force. They now have the key from the owners so they can drive off with the vehicle and not have to deal with all the security and manufacture's barriers.

This hot wiring thing, that's over, that's obsolete, now a days, and thieves will need a key to steal the vehicle in most cases. Thieves will look for their victims, they prefer a weak opponent, a weak victim.

So, you asked how a person can protect himself. They need to be alert, and mindful of their surroundings. Prevention is the key. The person who looks lively and is looking around, observant of its surroundings doesn't make a very good target for the thieves. These guys for the most part don't want a challenge.

Again, what people can do to protect themselves is a matter using common sense and listen to that little voice that tells you something is just not right. Familiarize yourself with what type of vehicles are more frequently stolen in your area, is your vehicle on the list? What are the chances of your car being stolen? Get to know what is going on in your town and neighborhood, what type of crimes occurred the most, where, when, and how. When out in the public, be alert, be familiar of your surroundings stay away from dark places at night, and avoid isolated areas.

As far as Law Enforcement and what is in stored for them, I

don't know. Technology is getting better every day and helping our officers, but the public needs to help. It has to be a partnership between the public, Law Enforcement, Law Makers and our courts.

Everyone giving and taking.

You know we have been talking about cars and trucks for the most part, but there is another type of theft. I'm talking about commercial theft, big rigs and their cargo. I'm referring to construction and farming equipment where one single unit is worth the equivalency of half a dozen cars or more. I'm talking about a $200,000.00 piece of equipment that nobody can believe it can, also be stolen. But, as the bartender in the movie, Irma La Duce used to say, "That's another story."

Chapter 15

Corruption within the Mexican ranks

A BM: *Ok next question is please talk about corruption in the police ranks in Mexico and how that affects fighting this major crime problem?

EC: You know Ricalday was not the only Mexican police officer that I befriended and that got killed. He was surely the one that possibly affected me the most. In total there were over a dozen, but he was special. We talked about family, we talked about corruption and he mentioned how he wanted to change things.

The week before he got killed he had been in El Paso along with his body guard and driver and we had gone to eat at Landry's which was real close to my office. We had talked about Victor and other commanders. He himself was questioning some of the methods that other Mexican Law Enforcement officers and Agencies took and he too, was concerned with corruption.

I mean, there were some guys like Dominquez who you kind of expect that something was going to happen someday, just a matter of time, but not Ricalday.

It is only fair to say that not ALL Mexican Police and officials are corrupt. Now, don't get me wrong, there are plenty.

Let me give you some examples of some people that I knew. Some died because they were corrupt, yet others died because they were not. But either way, when you have corruption in such a large scale, enforcing laws is very difficult.

Take for example guys like El Cowboy. El Cowboy was a *comandante* that came to take command of the auto theft unit of the Juarez State Police after Victor got killed. He was a strange one. He wasn't there but for about four months before he was killed. You know, when he first took over, I waited for about a week before I asked for a meeting with him. I wanted him to settle down first. Then I asked his supervisor, the Deputy Attorney General, if it was okay if I invited the new guy for breakfast so we could meet. The DAG (Deputy Attorney General) was kind of an okay guy. We got along good, never quite knew where he stood.

Of course I went through him so that the Commandant could not refuse me or post pone our meeting. If it came from his boss, he would have to meet with me.

I preferred to use this route instead of inviting him directly because of these two reasons. One, I wanted him to know that his boss was the one telling him to meet with me and two, his boss could tell him about me and my role. This also showed him that I had direct contact with his boss.

Anyway, we set up a breakfast meeting at the Holiday Inn on Lincoln Avenue in Juarez. I got there early and got a seat. I had already been told by some of his men that were close to me that he was kind of quiet and didn't speak much and they felt he was strange, he kept some distance and didn't seem to

ELIAS CAMACHO

trust anyone.

He arrived and I stood up and welcome him to our table. He was polite as he greeted me and he sat down. I was already having coffee and asked him if he wanted some and he said no. I asked him if he wanted to order something to eat, and he said no. This in its self, set me back, it's a no-no in Mexico. I mean this is being impolite and it's also unsociable not to accept an invitation to dine when it's obvious that, that was the reason we were coming together. We sat there for about 15 minutes and I did all the talking, very seldom would he say anything. He just listened as if he was there because he was told to be there, not that he wanted to be with me. His replies were mainly yes and no, but would not converse. Finally I paid and we both parted our separate ways.

I don't think he cared for me much. I talked to some of the guys later and explained what took place and they laughed. We kind of suspected that maybe he was in deep with some cartel, and it was not the local one. He was uncomfortable, as if out of place, mistrusting and unwilling to say much for fear of saying the wrong thing. I don't know if it was me (from the U.S.) or what I represented.

You know some of the best informants I had were the dispatchers. They knew everything about everybody. But by the same token, and because of that, they could be informants for the other side as well. What we sometimes referred to as "Brand X". I'll explain what I mean later.

Anyway, I wasn't able to be very productive while the Cowboy was in charge. We called him the cowboy because he always dressed in western attire. One day he was told to report to headquarters in Chihuahua City. The main headquarters in

Chihuahua is located close to a river that flows through the city and which has concrete all around. (Chihuahua is approximately 225 miles south from the border)

Next to the headquarters is a large parking lot for official vehicles. Once parked you can walk across the street to the main doors into the headquarters. Well, cowboy parked and was walking along the parking lot towards the street to across into the headquarters when a car drove up, pulled up next to him and two people stepped out and gunned him down just as he was standing by the parking lot. He didn't have a chance to react.

Somebody like that you sense from the beginning that it's just a matter of time for something to come down. He is obviously hiding something. I had been around enough to know that.

So you take care of yourself if you have any business with him, you make sure you do it inside an official building, you never go with him to socialize in certain public places. There could always be a stray bullet that could get you.

You know I mention dispatchers a few minutes ago. When it came to the auto theft unit here in Juarez, besides the commander the only person who could tell you where everybody was at, at any given time was the dispatcher. The auto theft unit had its own dispatcher separate from other investigative units. This guy not only kept track of everyone's movements, but he knew everyone's personal cell phone numbers, home address, and so forth. There were two main dispatchers and they weren't commission officers, they were more or less an apprentice who would eventually, if the commander so desired would become an agent.

When agent Saldaña and his partner were killed I always suspected that this particular dispatcher knew something. You see, I had known this dispatcher for some time, ever since he was about 16 years old. I first came across him about 4 years before Saldaña was killed. Saldaña himself had been a dispatcher some years earlier before becoming an agent.

This kid who was the dispatcher used to work for the owner of the towing company that I contracted with in Juarez. One day, I met this kid at the towing company's main office when I went to visit the owner. This shop besides vehicle repairs also did repairs to the wreckers, so they had a lot going on. Well, the owner introduced me to this kid telling me that the kid was a genius when it came to vehicle electronics. He could install and defeat just about any security system. He could unlock electronic door locks in cars, etc. He was somebody handy to have around at the wrecker company because often the need to open up or defeat an alarm system on a car before you towed it would be necessary.

The kid looked his age, not to tall, skinny and boyish looking with medium long brown hair. He looked friendly and seemed respectful and somewhat quite. This kid lasted working there for about two years and suddenly he was no longer there. I asked the owner of the tow company one day what had happened to the kid and he said he had moved on, and that was the end of that. I never asked the owner where he had gotten or how he met him. It was really none of my business. Just another employee.

About a year later the tow company owner called me to tell me that the commander of the Federal Highway Patrol in Juarez wanted to talk to both of us.

In its self, this was not strange, so I wasn't much concerned. So a day or so later we drove to the Highway Patrol headquarters on the outskirts of Juarez. I knew the commander, although I usually communicated and did most of our dealing with his 2nd in command. We were escorted into his office and found he was somewhat upset.

He first asked us if we knew so and so. I can't remember the name right now. At first I didn't know who he was talking about, the name didn't ring a bell, but the tow truck owner said "yes". I asked who they were referring to and the tow truck owner said they are talking about the kid that used to work at the lot and who was excellent with electronic systems. I definitely recalled him than and asked what was going on with him.

The commander informed us that he had just been arrested. He had stolen a car belonging to one of his agents and was stopped by another agent. The owner of the stolen vehicle had left his badge in the car and the kid had been going around flashing it at people. During interrogation the kid stated that he knew both of us and that actually he worked with us stealing cars! I said, "What, that's crazy we hardly know the kid, and stealing cars?" The commander insisted that we take care of the issue since that's what the kid was telling people.

We needed to be on alert! The commander said they had turned the kid over to the State Police for prosecution and he assume he would continue with this story about knowing us and so forth. "Okay", we said, "no problem", we thanked the commander and left.

The tow truck owner was embarrassed and apologized to me. He told me not to worry about it that he would go down to the State Police prosecutor's office and straighten everything out. I agreed and we parted different ways. I wasn't worried, I knew that kid had no creditability and besides they were lies and I was sure everyone knew it and it would blow away.

Times passed and I never ran into this kid again until about a year before Saldaña was killed. Victor was the commander at that time and I happen to see that same kid working as the dispatcher at Victor's auto theft office. I asked Victor, "What's is that kid doing here, do you know who he is?" Victor admitted he knew who he was and told me that he was hired by Human Resources and there was nothing he could do about it. I insisted that kid was no good, he is a car thief and who know what else. Victor just shrugged his shoulders and said, there is nothing I can do. Since I personally knew the lawyer who was in charge of operations and had a lot to do with human resources I went over to talk to her.

I said Graciela, I need to talk to you about one of your employees and I went ahead and told her what I knew about the kid. She seemed interested in what I had to say, but that kid continued there and was never removed. Somebody wanted him there.

One day Saldaña and his partner took into custody a new stolen Escalate which had been abandoned and which presumed owners later came to claim it. This kid was the dispatcher at the time, and it was with him with whom the presumed owners had come in to check to find out who were the officers that had taken the vehicle. The dispatcher contacted Saldana.

These guys had come over claiming the Escalate and after it was refused to them, the guys insisted to the point of threating Saldaña. Saldaña knowing it couldn't belong to the people who were claiming it, because it was stolen, told the guys to take a hike. They asked for the Commander and Victor also refused to release the Escalate. Saldaña and Victor were apparently suspicious of the guy's insistence and figured that there was something more to the vehicle. As I said before, usually the drug guys wouldn't make such a big hassle over a stolen vehicle, they would just let it go as part of doing business. Unless there was more to it. Something valuable in the vehicle.

I understand that Victor and Saldaña searched the vehicle and rumor has it that they found that the door panels were full of money. The vehicle must have been one of those that was being used to transport the drug money and Saldaña had messed things it up for them when he picked it up from the drop off point. That's probably what they guys were after, not the car per say.

Now, I don't know what happened to the money or the Escalate because we never got it back. Saldaña and his partner were gunned down weeks later as they drove their pick up unit in the city. Of course Victor was killed months later.

That kid later became an agent and he too was killed a few months after that. But I never trusted him.

So you can see how corruption can affect fighting major crime.

Chapter 16

The Common Denominator

A BM: * In this whole Crime situation the common denominator is *money*. Corruption is just one of the means to obtain it. People kill for it, people steal for it, people lie for it and people die for it. Corruption is something that is doing well everywhere, south American, Europe, Russia, in sports, in politics, it's found everywhere. But I guess if we have to pick on someone, let's pick on someone that's close and that's not us, Mexico.

EC: Yes, Mexico has a big problem with corruption and not just within Mexican law enforcement and politics, but in various other business transactions. And there is no doubt that money is at the root of it.

Corruption in Mexico goes all the way to the top. Funny though, many feel that if money, favors, or things are given to them without them asking for it, it's not corruption. It's something that is heavy woven into the fiber of its culture. It's something that the citizens knowing or unknowingly contribute to it.

I recall some years back reading a book on Cortez seven letters to the king. When Cortez explored and conquered Mexico all the explorers were required to give to the king a certain percentage of its valuable findings, gold, etc. Well, Cortez lied and did all kinds of maneuvers to keep more for himself and give less to the king. His reports were falsified. You might say that it all started with Cortez. It's something that was brought to Mexico and other Latin Countries from Europe.

Take a junior police officer regardless of the agency, fore the most part their salary is very, very low and they have little to no benefits at all and they serve at the pleasure of someone higher. So in order to make ends meet, he will need to find ways to supplement his earnings to feed his family. Job security is not a sure things as well as no retirement plan. Just like all of us, they want a better lifestyle, they want the nicer things life has to offer. But they can't get it with their salary. Since they can't get it with their poor salary, and easy money is offered to them, guess what? The individual officer becomes corrupt and accepts money.

In reality, in many cases, the money they get through their corrupted activities it's not just for them. It has been well documented that they have to share and shuffle money upwards towards higher ranks. This because the commander that's sitting in the office does not have the opportunity to be out in the street making money like the street cop does unless he is dealing with big dudes in other dirty businesses. And besides, the lower officer must keep his boss happy.

Therefore, it is expected and a duty of the junior officers to give it to him. Of course the more money an officer brings in the better he will be appreciated by his superiors. Someone who brings in no money, chances are will soon find himself out of a job soon enough.

On one occasion back in the med 80's I observed a State Commander during a shift change on a particular day when I had to go to Juarez. I had something very important and went real early in the morning. I was still working with the El Paso Police Department at the time as the Departments liaison officer. I was sitting there waiting for my Mexican counterpart to come in and report for the day shift. I sat next to the Commanders desk waiting. I noticed the commander had a big fish bowl on his desk top. I was pretty close to the big empty fish bowl and as the night shift was coming in to report the night's events before leaving for the day, they would approach the desk and throw crumpled dollar bills into the fishbowl. By the time I left that fish bowl was almost full. That bowl had more than just one dollar bills, some were of larger denominations, and I'm talking of twenties and larger. I jokingly told one of the guys later on, "Hey, how do I get a part or what?" That was a lot of money!

He then explained to me that the money was not all for the commander, most of it will go to the higher ups. "I didn't see YOU put any money in," he tells me laughing.

But you are right, it's all about money. I think I mentioned before that at an average I would spend 10 days out of the month in Mexico. Since I stayed at the same hotels and frequented the same restaurants and such, after a while people got used to seeing me. Due to this, especially when I was along, maybe having breakfast or coffee, they would start up a conversation. It usually started with a simple greeting and go from there. They knew I was an American and would frequently ask me questions. They all wanted to quit their jobs and come to the United States. They all knew someone or had a relative that had gone to the United States illegally and had had a very successful life. They seemed misinformed about many things. They were under the impression that once in the U.S. everything was going to be given to them or at least they were going to be given help and opportunities to get ahead in life.

They saw these friends and neighbors coming back for visits driving nice expensive cars and spending a lot of cash. And of course they wanted some of that. They all knew how to get someone to cross them across into the U.S. and get them a job. They knew what cities to go to and so forth. I would always tell them not to believe everything they heard and saw.

I would tell them to stay home and be content with what they had, greet was not good. But, it's all for the money. I don't know if the situation in Mexico will ever change.

As far as the drug situation goes, which is one of the main problem that contributes to a lot of what is happening in Mexico right now, I don't think see it ending anytime soon. No Mexican Municipal Police, State Police or Federal Police is ever going to be able to combat the drug cartels that are controlling everything at this time. They have a lot of money, more than the GDP of many countries.

You know I don't think that the Mexican Government is going to be able to do it alone. God, these cartels have a bigger budget that many countries. They've got enough money that some of them have offered to do away with the national debt if they are allowed to work without interruption.

These drug cartels must be looked at as we look at ISIS, they cannot be defeated by one country alone. It will take a combination of different fronts, they must be attacked not only physically, politically, but financially as well, and through any other means possible. It needs to be a group effort, not only Mexico, and the United States, but other countries as well. The drug problem is not a Mexico problem, it's not a U.S. problem, it's a world problem and as such it must be combated as such.

The supply will always be there if the demand is not stopped or curtailed. President Obama has just recently been giving pardons to people in prison who have been imprisoned for drug charges when they were not violent crimes. It seems it's because the punishment does not fit the crime. Some States are making marijuana legal.

The consumption needs to stop. The politician, lawyer, doctor, teacher, construction worker, and others who enjoy their leisure marijuana cigarette or dose of coke, have to, to some degree, assume some responsibility for the killings that have occurred and the corruption that is going on when it comes down to the drug cartels. Yes, the casual user also carries responsibility for the violence and crime that occurs due to the drug situation.

They might say they have no responsibility for this, it's not their doing, but if they did not smoke that cigarette or snuffed that cocaine, or shot up the heroine, there would be no need to combat the drugs.

If there is no demand, there is no sell, there is no need for supply, and it's that simple. Also if are going to fight the drug problem, we must let our law enforcement agencies do their work in combating these drug cartels. It's a war, and like any other war there is always going to be collateral damage. That's just the way it goes. Let's not do what we did with our military during the Vietnam War.

People are going to have to surrender certain amount of their liberty and stop being such crybabies. These soft hearted and do-gooders who are constantly crying out about civil rights, and who are constantly micro watching our police and second guessing our police actions, like Monday morning couch potatoe quarterbacks. I know and realize that police have to be kept accountable, but we can go overboard.

These drug cartels don't have ethics, nor scruples, they don't have to be politically correct, and they don't have rules or guide lines to work under. They don't work with the restrains that our police do. They are not scrutinize every time they turn around. Of course I don't mean to just let our police go wild, and do the things these drug dealers do, but we must loosen the leash a little. What good does it do for you to have a K-9 to protect your home and family when you are going to have him tied down with a huge chain in the back yard?

The U.S. should do the same thing they did with Columbia in the 1970's and tell Mexico, "No more money until you clear out your act." What do you need, move over, let us help.

It seemed to have somewhat worked in Colombia then, maybe it will work with Mexico now.

As far as Mexico is concerned and from another angle, I think that not until its citizens decide that it's time to pay their officers better salaries and give them benefits for their families, the corruption will not end. Officers need and to become more prepared by receiving proper education and training. Selection is very important. Officer positions should be competitive and officers should undergo intensive background check and interviews.

They also need to stop hiring people only because they are cousins or they are related one way or the other and hire a person because of their qualities not because of who they know. And most of all, make Law enforcement in Mexico a career not just a job. I believe that will help towards the ease of corruption in Mexico.

It's the citizen's responsibility to become involved on all levels. Unfortunately, this corruption is so embedded all the way to higher levels. I mean it's hard to tell how high, and our politicians don't believe it, they don't believe or don't want to believe that everybody out there is looking to rip from the benefits of corruption.

I don't know how this is ever going to be solved or if it's going to be solved at all. But I still say it's going to take the Mexican citizen and the general public, the masses, the tax payers, the house wife, the street sweeper, the store owner, the judge and everyone else to say, "Enough is enough", I will not feed this monster anymore. This monster is swallowing our youth, our future.

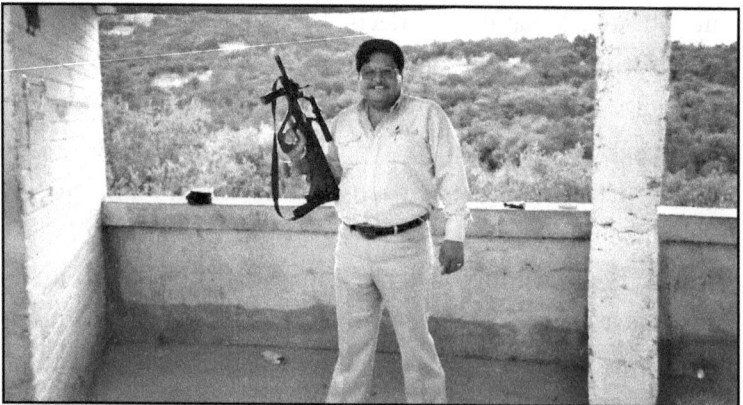

Author firearm pratice in Cuathemoc Chih. Mexico

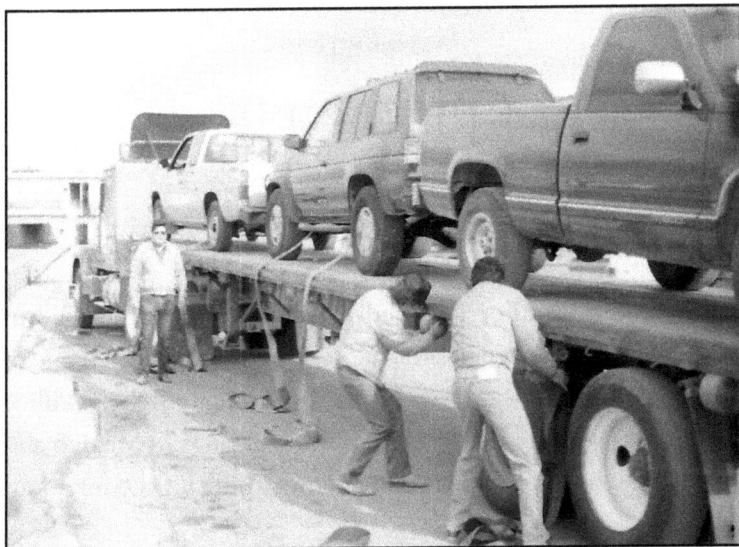

Author with vendors returning stolen vehicles to the U.S.

Author returning stolen heavy equipment from Mexico

EPILOGUE

Two months after I retired I had a call from the wife of Javier Licon (see photo chapter 7) . Javier had been one of my vendors in Juarez. Javier having been a State Judicial Police Agent was very knowedgeable of the workings in Mexico and was a great asset to me. He had been working for me for about 5 years.

Javiers wife called me to tell me that Javier had been killed. Javier had stopped at a neighborhood store to buy a beer on his way home and had been shot while sitting behind the steering wheel of his truck.

I checked further into it and learned that accodring to the owner of the store, Javier , as it was customery had come in and bought a beer and walked back to his truck which was parked across the street. Javier got in and behind his truck was another car. A man got out of the car and walked up to Javier and was talking to him through the drivers side window. The store owner saw when the man reached behind his back and pulled out a gun from his waist band and pointing at Javier point blank fired 2-3 times. Javier went down on the front seat and the man walked back to his car.

As the man was walking back to his car,he turned and saw that Javier was getting up, so the man walked back to the truck and again fired 2-3 more times through the open window makiing sure Javier was dead.

I later learned that it was all due to a Chyrsler 300 that we had recovered some time back and which was loaded with drugs.

Even up to the time of this writing, things have not changed in Mexico. People are still being killed in Mexico and there doesn't seem to be a bright look towards tomorrow. The comon denominator here is...Drugs and Money!

We talk about enforcment and incarceration ,but unless and untill we curtail the demand of these drugs in the United States, will there be a change. All of this is driven by our huge consumption and dependency on so called recreational drugs.